ENDURING
VALUES
IN A
CHANGING
SOCIETY

ENDURING
VALUES
IN A
CHANGING
SOCIETY

MARY J. McCORMICK

Family Service Association of America

New York

Contents

Foreword   vii

Introduction   1

1   Enduring Values in a Changing Society   3

2   Human Values and the Legal Perspective   32

3   The Democracy of Helping   68

4   The Role of Values in the Helping Process   95

5   The Role of Values in Social Functioning   114

6   Economic Dependency and the Social Services   135

7   Professional Responsibility and the Professional
    Image   162

8   Mary E. Richmond's Legacy of Values   182

For the medical profession as a whole this has apparently changed, no doubt because the social climate and broader value system in which the doctor is approved, privileged, and sanctioned have changed.

Another major theme underlying many of the following chapters is that although values have to do with the *ought* of human conduct, they ultimately are existentially grounded. The origin of values, almost like the laughing fox, eludes scholarly pursuit. But the search is important because values are major influencers of behavior. Why a people adopt one value orientation rather than another is simply an empirical and historical question. But whether a people should adopt one value orientation in preference to another is a normative question with ethical and philosophical implications and so drives the questioner to explore more deeply the nature of values and their philosophical as well as their empirical social and psychological origins. While recognizing that values have extensive cultural roots, McCormick holds, correctly I think, that the ethical and the existential are interrelated. What man and society ought to be rests, in some way, on what individual and social man is. Effective value systems manifest a reasonably good fit between the *ought* and the *is* of human affairs.

Dr. McCormick is experienced enough and has published enough on this subject to know that not all readers will accept all the assumptions she makes and the conclusions she reaches. The implication is that she put her hand to this current volume because of the recognized national need to rethink and reassess traditional American values. The recent notoriety given the unethical conduct of many in high places of government who flout those values shocked a nation that had perhaps become rather complacent about itself and its place in the world. Although she writes primarily for a social work audience, she illustrates her conceptualizations with material from law and medicine as well as the social sciences. What follows is timely and will stimulate discussion within many disciplines.

BERNARD J. COUGHLIN
President
Gonzaga University
Spokane, Washington

Introduction

Definitions of the word *values* range from the universal to the particular, from abstract principles to technical facts. Fortunately, one meaning among the many can be accepted as a common denominator—namely, the simple meaning of the Latin *valere,* "to be worth." This definition remains constant even when applied to such variables as time, place, and the human equation. Within the dimensions of worth, the shared values of democracy as an institution and social work as its instrument can be explored for their influence on the helping process as a mutual responsibility of the political and professional orders. In the present volume, human dignity is placed at the heart of a constellation of values, including personal identity, privacy and association, and choice and decision, which are both native endowments and constitutional privileges. They belong to the nature of man; they are recognized in the documents that shape the American way of life; they are per se the guidelines and the goals of professional help.

As these values are examined from such vantage points as philosophical backgrounds, legal perspectives, the giving and receiving of services, and the responsibilities of the helping professions, the urgency of their preservation becomes a recurring theme. This is the challenge which democracy and social work face in an era when people and events seem bent on destroying worth in all of its manifestations. Paradoxically, the defense against such destruction is tantamount to the values themselves; they are, at one and the same time, the means and the end of the struggle for survival. Fidelity to their dictates will not transform America into a utopia, but it will bring the nation closer to that certitude of thought and action which is the hallmark of a Judeo-Christian society and the birthright of its members.

1
Enduring Values in a Changing Society

Since its earliest days, social work in the United States has reflected the values of a democratic social order. Human dignity, personal autonomy (which implies personal responsibility), individual growth or self-fulfillment, and social experiences are the cornerstones of democracy and the focuses of the social services. Their importance to the Founding Fathers is apparent in the major documents that marked the birth of the nation. First, the Declaration of Independence identified the "self-evident" truths "that all men are created equal, that they are endowed by their Creator with certain unalienable rights, that among these are life, liberty and the pursuit of happiness." Later, the Articles of Confederation bound the states to a "firm league of friendship with each other for their common defense, the security of their liberties, and their mutual and general welfare." Finally, the Constitution was formulated and adopted "in order to form a more perfect Union, establish Justice, insure domestic

3

Tranquility, provide for the common defence, promote the general Welfare, and secure the Blessings of Liberty to ourselves and our Posterity."

A century and a half later, the United Nations, in its Universal Declaration of Human Rights, extended these principles to all its member countries. The wording of the Preamble is significant and strong: "Recognition of the inherent dignity and of the equal and inalienable rights of all members of the human family is the foundation of freedom, justice and peace in the world."[1] According to some commentators, the lasting value of the document lies in its emphasis upon the essential values of man as an individual and a social being. It renews, for today's world, the teachings of the philosophers of yesterday—notably Aristotle and Aquinas—who insisted upon this duality. The e pluribus unum concept becomes a practical reality; everyone, while maintaining his individuality, is a member of society and ipso facto "is entitled to realization . . . of the economic, social, and cultural rights indispensable for his dignity and the free development of his personality."[2] John W. Gardner states the principle and its implications with characteristic directness when he says, "To talk about individuality without talking about the social system that makes it possible is to talk nonsense."[3]

Individual Dignity and the Social Order

The individual human being, in his dignity and worth, stands at the heart of American democracy, a position which "rests exclusively upon the lively faith that individuals are beings of infinite value."[4] Democracy is the practical aspect of this assertion. As a political system, "it is predicated upon the measureless riches that arise from the variety of his [man's] inventiveness."[5] As a social system, its responsibilities are defined in the Bill of Rights, a document which, according to Henry W. Wriston, offers "dramatic and decisive proof of the primacy of the individual in our whole scale of values" and carries with it a commitment to the welfare of every citizen.[6] In line with this commitment, social work, as an instrument of society, "places the individual in the center of its concern."[7] Theoretically, there are no alternatives to this position, either in a democracy or in the social services. Practically, there may be options, but the difficulties of centrality are many; they present a continuous challenge because they continuously change.

The framers of the Constitution provided for this ongoing challenge by drawing up a document that was sufficiently adaptable in practice to permit such change. The Bill of Rights was destined to become a practical frame of reference within which the future, as well as the contemporary, citizen could examine and substantiate his position and his prerogatives. Perhaps there was a sprinkling of Yankee shrewdness in this move to avoid the dangers of what Winston Churchill described as the "cramping rigidity" of a written constitution. Perhaps these wise and dedicated men asked realistically the question posed rhetorically by Churchill: "What body of men, however farsighted, can lay down precepts in advance for settling the problems of future generations?"[8] Their answer, as it took shape in the first ten amendments, set the stage and the precedent for constitutional change.

The first of these amendments, adopted in 1791,

enjoys or suffers from—depending on one's point of view—unprecedented popularity, after two centuries, because it deals with the Four Freedoms. It seems valid to assume that never before have so many people so often appealed to the constitutional provision which places outside the law the unhampered exercise of religion, speech, peaceful assembly, and appeal. The wording of the text is explicit: "Congress shall make no law respecting an establishment of religion . . . or abridging the freedom of speech . . . or the right of the people peaceably to assemble, and to petition the Government." In these realms, the individual is in command; he can exercise, and even exploit, his individuality. More than that, he can demand the protection of society as he does so.

These basic safeguards are reinforced by the equally famous Fourth Amendment which establishes the "right of the people to be secure in their persons, houses, papers and effects." The Fifth Amendment extends this security to include protection against self-incrimination and double jeopardy. The next two amendments designate the means for implementing the preceding ones by providing "the right to a speedy and public trial" and "in suits at common law . . . the right of trial by jury" with the added protection against retrials. The Ninth Amendment makes it plain that the enumeration of these rights "shall not be construed to deny or disparage others retained by the people." The promise was not an idle one, and by 1974 there were twenty-six amendments in force.

Broad in scope and explicit in content, these provisions are characterized by what Justice Brandeis described as "great particularity." Their ideal and intent is "to protect Americans in their beliefs, their thoughts, their emotions and their sensations. They conferred, as against the Government, *the right to be let alone* [italics in original]—the most comprehensive of rights and the right most valued by civilized men."⁹ There can be no reasonable doubt about the mission of the Bill of Rights: to preserve the fundamental belief that "the dignity of the individual is the end, government only the means." To that end, both the social order and the social services must be able and willing to meet the challenge of social change without endangering the values that per se do not change. Nearly two hundred years have not weakened the purpose nor diminished the powers of the Bill of Rights. On the contrary, the famous declaration promises to thrust itself into the twenty-first century with all the vigor and purposefulness of the men who conceived it.

Values in the Social System

The unbroken connection between the individual and his milieu presupposes a social system in which he is the focus of all existing institutions—political, social, and economic. The primary objective of these institutions is to enhance his dignity, encourage his development or self-fulfillment, and protect his freedom. This objective can be accomplished only through balanced judgment about "the relative importance to be ascribed to the welfare of the state and to the welfare of its individual members."¹⁰ Wriston sees the maintenance of such balance as a fundamental dilemma, and obligation, of democracy because "when the general interest is overaccented, freedom declines and may disappear. . . . On the other hand, if individual interest utterly neglects social needs, anarchy is the end result. The consequence of either extreme is loss of liberty" and, it may be added, of human dignity.[11]

The extremes are avoided only when the common culture that emerges is a true expression of the basic values of a given society. As this emergence takes place, values become optional. They can be accepted or rejected, denied or confirmed, by individuals, groups, and courts of law. If the possibility of challenge had no limits, the results could be catastrophic to the extent that unity would be threatened or destroyed. Fortunately for man and society, the danger is averted as values take on a regulatory role in which criteria applicable to the whole of living, individual and social, are established and actualized. Moreover, these criteria carry sanction: The rule of law comes into play and society is made responsible for its enforcement. This is essential because the rule itself constitutes man's protection against violation, real or potential, of his dignity and freedom.

The completion of this cycle brings with it both certitude and challenge. Values continue to be optional to the extent that they can be legitimately questioned. At the same time, they can be relied on to supply the norms and standards which, in a sense, control the challenge and lend some degree of security to otherwise insecure performances. More than this, they are the ties that join human beings to each other and to the social order; they literally hold a nation together. To quote Gardner again, these shared values, with their accompanying beliefs and attitudes, bring to a nation "its tone, its fiber, its integrity, its moral style, its capacity to endure."[12] Perhaps because their function is so dynamic, it is sometimes easy to lose sight of the fact that values are abstractions, not objects of sensory perception. The impact that Gardner describes is the work of their effects—the goals, the motivations, and the behavior patterns that arouse the senses and bring responses from living, feeling, acting human beings.

Because these responses, whether individual or collective, come from its members, society, as an entity, is placed in a position of responsibility toward those members. It must respond to their needs, wants, and wishes, whether in the direction of preserving or of changing the status quo. The chain of events, once set in motion, may be constructive or destructive, reason-oriented or emotion-dominated. The fact remains that, either way, values are at stake and society must act to protect the good or eradicate the evil. Its overall responsibility extends beyond the social good to the social ills—the suffering, the poverty, the discrimination, the disasters—that are by their very nature a contradiction of values.

Values in Social Work

In the Western world in general, and in the United States in particular, this responsibility is discharged, in part, through the welfare policies, programs, and institutions that lend themselves to the practices of social work. The values implicit in the theories and methods of social work supply the common bond between the individual who is the focus of service and the social order in which that service takes on form and substance. Social work thus becomes an instrument of the social order; its values complement and supplement the values that are society's heritage and strength and on which its chances for survival depend.

If this analysis is accepted, the values of social work as a helping process can be said to originate in the values of a democratic social order. They can be examined within the single conception which, according to Gardner, is "central to the consensus" in that order—namely, the dignity and worth of the individual. The derivative values then become identifiable as ones which support that dignity—personal autonomy, which embraces personal freedom; self-fulfillment, which "is placed at the summit";[13] and interaction, on which "all that makes us most human" depends.[14] These are the old familiar concepts. Within the new dimensions of the 1970s, they seem to take on different, even contradictory, meanings but, if Robert W. Kelso's observation of fifty years ago is accepted, the differences are transitive rather than substantive. In addressing the National Conference of Social Work in 1922, he said, "The basic truths of human existence do not change. . .[although man's] conception of them is always changing."[15] If this statement is correct, then the seeming dichotomy between the old and the new is traceable to man's thinking about, and attitude toward, values, not to the values themselves.

The significant point is that the conceptual change which has gained prominence fifty years after Kelso spoke is a fact of life and, as such, demands recognition, if not necessarily acceptance. Essentially, its focus is the concept of social worth in contrast to individual worth. The former implies a kind of egalitarianism that tends to submerge the uniqueness of the human being and give precedence to his social qualities. His role in society can be likened to that of a single link in an endless chain formed of identical links. His real worth stems from his potential as one among many, not as one.

Within this frame of reference, derivative values reflect the emphasis on the social or collective side of man's nature and shift the priorities that democracy accords him as an individual. In the interests of a working terminology, these derivatives can be designated as social autonomy, in which individual decision-making, and all that it implies, gives way to the decisions of the group. Self-development then becomes identified with development in community. Social activism, with its focus on the collective, seems to replace social interaction, with the individual at its center. The question then is: What happens to the theory and practice of social work, as well as to democracy, when old values are challenged or discarded and new ones threaten to take their place? The answer is fairly obvious: Both the old and the new are, at one and the same time, defended and condemned, battle lines are drawn, and fragmentation is the inevitable result.

The analysis that follows constitutes an attempt to find an antidote for this hazard by proposing a framework within which social work can be examined in its relationship to its own values and to those of American democracy. If this framework is accepted, it follows that the values of social work will be in doubt only if democracy shares the same fate. Their preservation depends, therefore, on a joint effort, not to find new values but to strengthen commitment to the old. This does not imply rigidity; on the contrary, it denotes the flexibility that takes into account changes in man's ideas about values and his sense of responsibility toward them. The changes come with each new era in the life of a people and a nation and with each new stage in the development of a profession.

Constructive action in the face of such change becomes a mutual obligation of society in general and of social work in particular. The key to its success is balance. Both social work and the social order must avoid the extremes that are equally disastrous: casting out the old with few, if any, reservations or embracing the new with a comparable lack of restraint. Each must recognize the strength of its own heritage as it copes with present realities and future uncertainties, even as it launches innovations which, for all practical purposes, are without precedent. The success of the outcome, so far as values are concerned, depends primarily on a reasonable balance between the supremacy of individual worth, as highlighted in the nation's credo, and the enhancement of social worth as manifested in the extension of that credo in the interest of the common good. This is the real challenge to values—the one that calls for continuous exercise of judgment and will, the one on which the survival and permanence of social work and its values depend.

Social Work and Individual Worth

During the early years of America's development, social work found its place as an instrument of service within the context of these demands. At the beginning of the

twentieth century, Mary E. Richmond gave it a particular
form in the individualized approach of casework. Out of
fifteen years of learning and experience, she presented,
in *Social Diagnosis,* perhaps the earliest authoritative statement of the aim and method of social casework as the
"betterment of individuals or families, one by one, as
distinguished from their betterment in the mass."[16] She
recognized the fact that individuals and masses are inter-
dependent and, therefore, that social reform and social
casework must progress together. However, individual
differences comprise the focal point from which casework takes its direction and develops its technique. Her
rationale is worth quoting: "In the early stages of a
democracy [and, conceivably, of the helping process]
doing the same thing for everybody seems to be the best
that administrative skill is equal to, but later we learn to
do different things for and with different people with
social betterment clearly in view."[17] These "different
things" pointed the way to the principles and methods of
the individualized approach that identified Richmond's
concept of social work.

The concept, in viable form, was destined to gain
strength and popularity during the 1920s as casework
joined forces with psychology and psychiatry in a
renewed emphasis on the individual. The readiness of
social workers to follow, even though sometimes con-
fused by, the dictates of these disciplines is too familiar
to warrant elaboration here. For the caseworker of the
1920s, helping became therapy, objectivity became the
watchword, and the highly individualized professional
relationship became the distinguishing mark of service.
Insofar as these new directions contributed to individual
betterment, they could not be faulted. There was, how-

ever, an element of risk. If, at any time, sophisticated techniques became more important than sympathetic responses and if human needs were submerged in scientific explanations, then social workers were in danger of losing that power of sympathy which Richmond described in 1890 and which Gordon Hamilton reemphasized fifty years later.[18] To Richmond, it was an "indispensable quality"; to Hamilton it was a "special kind of love" or "acceptance." In the minds of both, it connoted the desire and the ability of the social worker to help another person to cope with his own needs in the interests of his own well-being.

Whether or not the commitment was actually endangered in the 1920s is a matter of speculation; that it was threatened in the 1930s is a historical fact. Mass poverty, breadlines, enforced idleness, and inevitable frustration penetrated every social group at all economic levels. The consequent hazards to human dignity and the constant pressures on human resources—persons, agencies, finances, manpower—were only too familiar to those who fought their way through the Depression years. In the course of the battles, every conceivable defense— from hostility and defiance to apathy and helplessness— became a weapon in the hands of those who were discouraged, if not defeated, by the turn of events. It would have been easy, perhaps even expedient, for social workers to ignore the individualized meaning of responses that so rapidly became generalized. Perhaps some of them did. But, to the lasting credit of the profession, there were many who, with Bertha C. Reynolds, remained firm in their allegiance to human dignity and its protection.

Out of a wealth of experience as practitioner, educator, and research specialist, Reynolds early reminded her colleagues that "at the very heart of our work are the human beings with whom we deal." This is one of "the things that cannot be shaken," even when the "cherished routine" of sound administration, skillful interviewing, and planned treatment give way to the urgency of common human needs.[19] At the mid-point of the Depression, with federal legislation as yet untested, she again reminded social workers of the supreme value of the individual "in a world which seems, by blundering if not by design, to hold human life as the cheapest of commodities."[20] Forty years later, the words have an ominous meaning as social work perseveres in the service to human beings who are threatened by the system of the 1970s rather than the Depression of the 1930s. The current threat to individual dignity comes, not from poverty or unemployment or racism per se but from negation of the values that men and women have been taught to cherish.

During the post-Depression years and continuing through the 1960s, private agencies reassessed their functions in the light of these threats. Following the period in which psychoanalytic orientation prevailed, these agencies moved toward a renewed focus on human needs in the aggregate and extended their services beyond the highly selective clientele of the early 1950s. In doing so, they reached out to a cross-section of people whose problems presented a combination of personal and social factors. The dynamics of frustration became just as apparent in student revolts and acts of civil disobedience as they were in individual unemployment or mental illness or statutory crime.

Agencies early discovered that coping with these

multidimensional situations required a kind of double vision. The difficulties of a single individual had to be weighed in the present and, whenever possible, corrected. These same difficulties, as well as the proposed solutions, had to be projected into the future and examined in terms of long-range implications. The challenge was to act in the best interests of the future, within the context of the present and against the background of the past. The correlation is not new; the greatest philosophers of the thirteenth century recognized its validity. In his analysis of human actions, Aquinas wrote: "The past has become a kind of necessity, since what has been done cannot be undone. In like manner, the present as such has a kind of necessity [it is the now] . . . consequently, future contingencies, insofar as they can be directed by man to the end of human life" are the bases of constructive action. The syllogistic reasoning has held firm through the centuries; the twenty-first is not likely to disturb it.

Meanwhile, public welfare programs "administered by humans for humans" were expanded under the Social Security Act in line with "the significant principles which make for sound individualization in a program based on right."[21] These developments extended into areas as diversified as child welfare and rehabilitation, medical care and manpower. Jane M. Hoey saw in them "an expression of a democracy's concern that its human resources be conserved, that opportunities for self-development and contribution to family and community life be safeguarded."[22] In other words, they became an added expression of the aim and purpose of social work as an instrument of the social order, an instrument which, it was hoped, would be shared by public and private agencies in their mutual concern for human needs as well as for human rights. This sharing could be realized only if governmental programs maintained the kind of "identity with people" which, to quote Charlotte Towle, depends on "a basic understanding of individuals, a growing comprehension of their common needs, of their behavior motivations, and of the factors and forces which shape men to socialized and unsocialized ends."[23] In 1945, Towle expressed the hope that such understanding would lead to the formulation of policies that would adequately interpret the intent of the Social Security Act.

Against this background, the body politic moved into the sociolegislative changes that were to make history in the 1960s. The keynote was sounded in the Civil Rights Act of 1957. This act encompassed a constitutional definition of those personal rights that were made specific in the subsequent acts of 1960 and 1964. In combination, these measures provided injunctive relief against discrimination in places of public accommodation, desegregation of public facilities and public education, nondiscrimination in federally assisted programs, and equal employment opportunities. This legislation was climaxed in the Voting Rights Act of 1965, which strengthened the Fifteenth Amendment and the powers of Congress to enforce it. In the language of the law, the prerogatives of the franchise "shall not be denied or abridged by the United States or by any State on account of race, color or previous condition of servitude." Protection was thereby assured to all citizens "in the conditions of political and social behavior." The manifestos of the early years were thus projected onto the contemporary scene, and their permanency was once again substantiated.

This was the pattern at the beginning of the 1970s

as social work—partly from choice and partly from necessity—consciously assumed a double identity. Traditional
responsibility for persons was extended to innovative
responsibility for people; activities in the interest of the
individual were complemented by action in the interest
of society. There is no point in evading the difficulties
which these changes have posed, both in principle and
practice. In the former, the ensuing problems may, on
examination, be more apparent than real; in the latter,
they are both apparent and real. The growing commitment to the social component in rights and needs has
become a direct challenge to the long-time allegiance to
individual human beings. The issues at stake are complicated. It is possible, however, to identify certain aspects of the challenge which are pertinent to social work
in its role of fostering both individual betterment and
social well-being.

Social Work and Social Worth

Because man is a social as well as an individual being, his
values extend beyond himself as an isolated entity and
into his relationships with other men. The quest for personal development leads him into an ever-widening cir-
cle of associations ranging from family and peers to community, in its broadest sense. The significance of this
activity has been recognized by speculative philosophers
and empirical scientists as widely separated as Aristotle
and Charles Darwin. To such authorities and their followers, the social component in man's nature is as vital

to his well-being as the individuality which he cherishes. The crucial factor is balance. Neither must be permitted to overshadow, much less destroy, the other because together they hold the key to effective living. Paul Tillich updated this concept for contemporary minds when he wrote: "Only in the continuous encounter with other persons does the person become and remain a person. The place of this encounter is the community."[24] Gardner is more explicit. In his judgment, "the mature person must . . . come to terms with his membership in the society at large and give his allegiance to values more comprehensive than his own needs." This interaction is imperative because he is not sufficient unto himself. His relationship with "values that lie beyond the self . . . is an essential ingredient of the inner strength that must characterize the free man."[25] In other words, the individual human being must preserve, but not be limited by, his own values. He must find a place for the values of others. This thinking is, in essence, the philosophical background against which democracy as an institution and social work as an instrument must approach, and cope with, rights and needs in their characteristic patterns of uniqueness and commonality.

Prior to the early 1960s, social work in general and casework in particular emphasized the uniqueness part of the equation. The total process was one of individualization, with the personal element dominant and personal growth as the major objective. This orientation, formulated by Richmond and strengthened by the definitions of the Milford Conference, plus substantive content from psychology and psychiatry, coalesced into the clinical model. Based on the medical concept of pathology, the model gained wide acceptance in the helping professions. Because its focus was on the individual whose problems were interpreted as dominantly psychogenic, the resulting methodology was readily adaptable to psychology, psychiatry, and social work. Each of these disciplines viewed such a person as sick and, therefore, in need of treatment. His specific difficulties might encompass the material needs with which social workers are familiar, but cause and effect were explored and treated against the background of the personal or emotional, rather than the social, component. The entire process was highly individualized and the potentials for cure were sought in man, not in society.[26]

These premises were open to challenge. The social reforms of the early 1900s and the social conscience from which they sprang rejected, at least implicitly, the pathological element in diagnosis and treatment. If there was pathology, it was as readily identifiable with such institutions as law, education, and industry as with persons. Human betterment was contingent on factors common to society as well as those specific to persons. This thesis furnished the basis for a model in which the person and society were complementary points of reference and the treatment of social ills equaled in importance the cure of personal illness. The common problems of the social order were thus placed in balance with individual reactions, and both sets of factors were recognized for their influence on man's present and future progress.

This interrelationship and its impact on social worth have been supported, in substance, by American sociologists from the early days of the reformers who were interested in social problems per se to the present-day theorists who focus on those problems within the spectrum of social systems. At the turn of the century, Lester

F. Ward expressed the belief that the "evils that individuals suffer are often due to the constitution of [the] society which entails them" and which, through its own inertia, fails "to keep pace with the growth of the living mass within it." The impact of such failure is bound to be far-reaching because human beings purposefully shape their own destinies through "a perfection of social mechanisms and institutions."[27] Without such instruments and the interchange that accompanies their use, both personal development and social progress are blocked and social worth is correspondingly diminished. Each must keep pace with the other if the whole is to remain in balance.

The dynamics of this interchange received a more sophisticated kind of support from Robert K. Merton and his colleagues in the 1960s when they stressed the importance of "articulation between psychological and social studies" in such areas as family disorganization, crime, alcoholism, and drug addiction. They argued that sociological analysis requires "the use of a general theory of personality and knowledge of the distinctive personality characteristics of participants in the [social] system as a whole or in major subsystems, and in particular roles." This theory does not imply a "reduction of sociological analysis to the presumably more basic level of psychological analysis." It simply means "an integration or coordination of two basic sets of data" and recognition of their unified impact on human action, both immediately and in the long view.[28]

During this same period of time, leaders in social work, from pioneers to professionals, recognized the social aspects of human needs and society's responsibility to do something about them. To Jane Addams and her co-workers, for example, it was not enough to offer the multiple services of Hull House. These must be supplemented by action directed toward correction or prevention of the conditions which made the services necessary. Day-care programs were important but so was membership in the National Child Labor Committee or the National Committee for Mental Hygiene. It was important to give immigrant mothers instruction in child care and it was equally important to secure, as Jane Addams did, an appointment as city sanitation inspector, the better to fight in the political arena for community health programs. In the minds of these highly motivated men and women, social work that was truly social could not be restricted to the relief of material needs on a personal basis. It must extend itself to the idea of raising life to its highest value—namely, the individual dignity and social worth of every human being.

It remained for Nathan E. Cohen and his associates, in the early 1960s, to formulate and test these concepts at a different level of abstraction. In the problem-oriented model described in *Social Work and Social Problems,* the authors fully recognize the importance of the individualized approach and the clinical orientation. They contend, however, that social work can not justifiably confine itself to a unilateral methodology because, as an instrument of society, its responsibilities extend to social institutions and policies in their present and future implications. It is therefore imperative that the analysis of any problem be conducted within a multidimensional frame of reference. The resulting model stresses the intrinsic, complementary relationship between the individual and the social order. It reinforces the belief in man's worth as a human being whose needs and values reflect both his socialization and his individuality.[29]

The rapid, sometimes unprecedented, and often dramatic, social changes of the late 1960s undoubtedly served as a catalyst in shaping another approach to this duality—namely, the advocacy model.[30] Oriented to the plight of the disadvantaged, this model emphasized the responsibility of social work "for a social order in which the individual has a better chance of not being defeated"[31] and in which his social worth becomes the focus of development. Intervention, in the sense of interference that may affect the interests of others, both immediately and in the future (rather than reform in the hope of restoring a past condition or revitalizing a present one), is the watchword. This leads to a new image in which activism is the dominant theme. On first appraisal, both concept and image may seem revolutionary; on examination, they reflect the principles of the early reformers and the methods of the pioneers. Advocacy, as applied to contemporary social work did not spring, like Athena, from the head of Zeus; it had its forebears. Like Zeus, however, it became the father of many gods, and herein lies the anomaly.

The word *anomaly* is used advisedly here, in the sense of deviation from prevailing patterns of service. This deviation became evident, very early, in the intense commitment to innovation and adaptation. Social agencies, irrespective of fields or specializations, were faced with direct involvement in "bold, new creative programs designed to meet the larger challenge of affirmative social action"; they were called upon to consolidate their resources in mass attacks against "the hostile environment which contributes so much to the personal ills to which social workers address themselves."[32] This environment might bring deprivation in the area of common human needs or through the infringement of human rights, or it might present a constellation of problems as widely diversified as those of the inner city and Appalachia. Whatever the hazards, their existence leads to a new emphasis on man's social worth and on the responsibility of social work to man in society.

In meeting this responsibility, structured agencies were confronted with basic changes in administration and operation. Flexibility became the criterion of success in both areas. New demands called for new services implemented through the use of strategies adaptable to the marketplace as well as to the clinic, to people in the aggregate, and to problems that were universal. It was of primary importance that these services be readily available, to be used or not used by those to whom they were delivered, without reference to formalized diagnostic and treatment procedures. It was equally important that the strategies adopted should come within the competence of paraprofessional and nonprofessional as well as indigenous personnel, who were free to apply them without reference to administrative or professional restrictions. The focal point of the total process was social betterment through the enhancement of social worth. The advocacy model, in toto, brings a new dimension to social work in the 1970s and promises a new direction to the social work of the future.

The Human Equation: Rights, Needs, Values

Whether the model which prevails at any given time is clinical, problem-solving, or interventive, it is founded, in principle, on the democratic ideals that surround human dignity. This means that social work in the role of instrument, strives by any methods consistent with its own principles of service, to bring about a reconciliation between the rights of man, the needs of man, and the values from which each of them springs. These are the essentials of the human equation; they must be recognized in their cohesive relationship if the profession hopes to fulfill both its public trust and its individual commitment to the present and future well-being of society and its members.

Recognition of these essentials should not be difficult: The parts of the equation are easy to identify. Rights are the constant factors; needs are the variables or the unknowns; values represent the equality sign that, placed between the two, should stabilize them in relation to each other and to the individual and social character of human beings. Theoretically, this stabilization is the common objective of democracy and of social work. Practically, its attainment has become a perennial challenge to both the body politic and the helping professions. The reasons are complex. However, some facts emerge which tend to clarify the persistent dichotomy between the rights man cherishes, the needs he experiences, and the values that account for the impact of each on himself and on the social order.

The basic fact is that rights are legally defined and protected; needs, even when socially identified, are not ipso facto within the letter of the law. This difference in status is apparent in the history of American democracy, from the town meetings of colonial days to the Supreme Court sessions of the 1970s. Rights are venerable; they are treated objectively and, if challenged, can be defended as essential to the security of the people and the state. The rule of law is their safeguard. Needs, on the other hand, bring less affirmative action. They are vulnerable and, even though as old as man, they seem always to be without precedent. Consequently, society tends to ignore them until a real or impending crisis demands attention. Even then, the response is apt to be indecisive and emotionally charged as solutions intended for the masses are tried and found wanting in the face of individual differences. Democracy becomes trapped, once again, in the age-old dilemma of how to preserve individual rights and meet personal needs and, simultaneously, maintain the sense of community which is essential to the total picture.

At this point, values play a distinctive role insofar as they account, with equal certainty, for the rights that are the foundations of American democracy and the needs that are the subjects of American social work. Human dignity and its accompanying values, as the operative principles in each, are not new; they have withstood the test of time; they have not changed in the face of social change. Man's dignity was recognized with equal decisiveness in the Mosaic laws with their passion for justice and in the Christian Gospels with their passion for charity. The modern mind recognizes the continuum as Gardner describes it:

> The idea of a society embodying some or all of these values is hardly new. Down the generations, a great many men and women have worked, dreamed, suffered, waited, struggled and sacrificed to contribute to the grand design of that society.[33]

At every stage of the world's history, these same men and women:

> pour out torments [*sic*] of words about the values they wish to live by, and lo, they turn out to be, for the most part, updated versions of very old values. True, the values have been ignored, traduced, lied about, manipulated, and falsified. But that only says that they need rescuing.[34]

Gardner then suggests that the first step in the rescuing process is the rediscovery of values in one's own tradition. He maintains, *"Our problem is not to find better values but to be faithful to those we profess* [italics in original]." This fidelity is expressed in social action—that is, by doing "the sometimes necessary, sometimes expensive, often complicated things" that are the responsibility of a social order designed to protect the rights and meet the needs of human beings. Each of these obligations is dependent on the other. Rights can be preserved only if the accompanying needs, whether material or psychological, are treated so as to prevent social disaster and personal damage. If this dual purpose is to be accomplished in a society that continuously reexamines and reinterprets both, then values must be respected as the stabilizing forces. They alone represent the "core of conscious conviction" and the "truth that man doesn't have to keep reminding himself is true." Gardner repeatedly drives home the fact that values must not come, as they so often do these days, "with question marks attached."[35] On the contrary, they must bring, to democracy and to social work, the kind of certitude that is the intent of the Bill of Rights and the raison d'être of the helping professions.

NOTES

1 United Nations, *Universal Declaration of Human Rights,* preamble, final authorized text, 1948; reprinted April 1968.

2 Ibid., article 22.

3 John W. Gardner, *Self-Renewal: The Individual and the Innovative Society* (New York: Harper & Row, 1965), pp. 86–87.

4 Henry M. Wriston, "The Individual," in *Goals for Americans: Report of the President's Commission on National Goals* (Englewood Cliffs, N.J.: Prentice-Hall, 1960), p. 49.

5 Ibid., p. 53.

6 Ibid., p. 37.

7 Harriett M. Bartlett, *The Common Base of Social Work Practice* (New York: National Association of Social Workers, 1970), pp. 65–69.

8 Winston Churchill, *History of the English-Speaking Peoples,* ed. Henry Steele Commager (New York: Dodd, Mead, 1965), p. 292.

9 Quoted by Wriston, "The Individual," in *Goals for Americans,* p. 37.

10 Alfred North Whitehead, *Adventures of Ideas* (New York: Macmillan, 1933), p. 50.

11 Wriston, "The Individual," in *Goals for Americans,* p. 48.

12 John W. Gardner, *The Recovery of Confidence* (New York: Pocket Books, 1971), p. 93.

13 Wriston, "The Individual," in *Goals for Americans,* p. 48.

14 Gardner, *Self-Renewal,* p. 91.

15 Robert W. Kelso, "Changing Fundamentals of Social Work," in *Readings in Social Case Work, 1920–1938,* ed. Fern Lowry (New York: Columbia University Press, 1939), pp. 3, 4.

16 Mary E. Richmond, *Social Diagnosis* (New York: Russell Sage Foundation, 1917), p. 25.

17 Ibid., pp. 367–68.

18 Mary E. Richmond, "The Friendly Visitor," in *The Long View,* ed. Joanna C. Colcord and Ruth Z.S. Mann (New York: Russell Sage Foundation, 1930), p. 41; and Gordon Hamilton, *Psychotherapy in Child Guidance* (New York: Columbia University Press, 1947), pp. 126–27.

19 Bertha C. Reynolds, "The Things That Cannot Be Shaken," *The Family,* 13 (April 1932): 51–54.

20 Bertha C. Reynolds, "Social Case Work: What Is It? What Is Its Place in the World Today?" *The Family,* 16 (December 1935): 235–42.

21 Charlotte Towle, *Common Human Needs*, Public Assistance Report no. 8 (Washington, D.C.: U.S. Government Printing Office, 1945), p. vii.

22 Jane M. Hoey, "Foreword," in *Common Human Needs*, p. iii.

23 Towle, *Common Human Needs*, p. vii.

24 Paul Tillich, *The Courage to Be* (New Haven, Conn.: Yale University Press, 1965), p. 91.

25 Gardner, *Self-Renewal*, p. 92.

26 John M. Romanyshyn, *Social Welfare: Charity to Justice* (New York: Random House, 1971), pp. 357–58; and Bartlett, *The Common Base of Social Work Practice*, pp. 32–33.

27 Israel Gerver, ed., *Lester Frank Ward. Selections from his Work* (New York: Thomas Y. Crowell Company, 1963), pp. 10–12.

28 Alex Inkeles, "Personality and Social Structure," in *Sociology Today*, ed. Robert K. Merton et al. (New York: Harper & Row, 1965), 2: 272–73; and Robert K. Merton, "Epilogue: Social Problems and Sociological Theory," in *Contemporary Social Problems*, 3rd ed., ed. Robert K. Merton and Robert A. Nisbet (New York: Harcourt Brace Jovanovich, 1971), pp. 793–845.

29 Nathan E. Cohen, ed., *Social Work and Social Problems* (New York: National Association of Social Workers, 1964), pp. 362–91.

30 Mary J. McCormick, "Social Advocacy: A New Dimension in Social Work," *Social Casework*, 51 (January 1970): 3–11.

31 Theodora L. Wilson, "Social Work from the Perspective of Fifty Years: A Personal History," *Smith College Studies in Social Work*, 42(February 1972) :114.

32 Ibid., p. 113.

33 Gardner, *The Recovery of Confidence,* p. 95.

34 Ibid., p. 94.

35 Ibid., pp. 89–98.

MARY J. McCORMICK was for many years associate professor of casework and research at the School of Social Work, Loyola University of Chicago. Then, from 1959 until she was named professor emeritus in 1974, she served as professor in the sociology department and director of the undergraduate curriculum in social welfare at the University of San Francisco.

She has held memberships for many years in the National Association of Social Workers and the Council on Social Work Education and has served on various local and national committees. In 1965, as a member of the Commission on Social Work Ethics of NASW, Dr. McCormick edited that commission's report, issued as *The Social Workers' Code of Ethics: A Critique and Guide.* In collaboration with David E. Tannenbaum and an appointed task force, she edited the document "Dimensions of Social Work Values in the United States: Implications for Social Work Education," which was published in 1969 in *International Social Work.* Her writings have also appeared in *Social Casework, Journal of Education for Social Work,* and *Social Service Review,* and she has published two previous books: *Thomistic Philosophy in Social Casework* and *Diagnostic Casework in the Thomistic Pattern.*

2
Human Values
and the
Legal Perspective

In a simple rhetorical question, Jacques Maritain joined human rights and human values. "How then can one claim rights if one does not believe in values?" He assumed the answer and offered the rationale. "If the affirmation of the intrinsic value and dignity of man is nonsense, the affirmation of the natural rights of man is nonsense also."[1] In other words, if man possesses value and dignity, then he also possesses the inalienable rights that surround these qualities and the derivative rights that support them. The former were identified by the Founding Fathers as self-evident truths; the latter were probably taken for granted by these men of deep conviction about and trust in their fellowmen. In a generation less dedicated and less trusting, however, confidence gives way to skepticism and challenge becomes a cause célèbre. As Robert Frost wrote, "there's always something to be sorry for,/A sordid peace or an outrageous war." He went on to say that there are always those who try "to grasp with too much social fact/Too large a situation."[2]

Perhaps this comment is the crux of the ongoing dilemma about values and rights. Rooted in the past, interpreted in the present, and vindicated only in the future, they may indeed comprise too large a situation to be comprehended. If so, a shift of focus from the whole to its component parts might be the beginning of wisdom. Life, liberty, and the pursuit of happiness represent the whole. These are the universals and they are abstractions; they become concrete only in day-by-day experiences specific to time, place, and person. The movement from the general to the particular is marked by the emergence of other values that are operational in character and have their own identity and function. These derivative values and their correlative rights influence every aspect of life in a democratic society. They account for the ways in which human beings react to themselves, for example, in the event of success or failure; to other persons through individual and group relationships; to the social order through conformity or dissent. Man's behavior in these areas testifies to his fidelity to, or negation of, the personal and social values and rights that bring meaning and direction to the challenge of living.

Maritain points out that both the values and the rights "are inalienable since they are grounded on the very nature of man, which of course no man can lose." However, he qualifies this truth as applied to rights since, while their possession is beyond dispute, at least in a democracy, their exercise is debatable. Although generic to the nature of society and the individual, these rights become specific when applied to the interests of each; they can be exercised to the advantage or detriment of either party. For this reason, it is imperative that rights be made subject to the conditions of justice—that is, to the order and rule which assure the protection of the individual and the common good. This assurance is realized when justice operates through the rule of law and the order of the judiciary. It is only through these instruments that society can legitimately intervene in the interests of its members. Such intervention does not infringe on the possession of rights; it simply restricts the ways in which that possession can be exercised.

By way of illustration, Maritain applies this reasoning to the rights to life and to the pursuit of happiness. Since these rights are inviolate, "the common good would be jeopardized if the body politic could restrict in any measure the possession that men naturally have of them." Nevertheless, some human beings deprive themselves—and are consequently deprived by society—of their exercise. The criminal who has violated the mandates of justice retains the generic rights to life and happiness. By his actions, however, he has jeopardized the specific rights—security, communication, privacy—through which the universal becomes particular in the social order. When this happens, the state, as the organized will of society, either wholly or partially curtails the rights, and the person can no longer exercise them at his own discretion. According to Maritain's reasoning, it is mandatory that the state do so, since both justice and the common good are endangered if the body politic fails to protect its members against real or potential danger.[3]

The derivative rights which spring from the basic tenets of democracy and, therefore, demand society's protection, are those of corporate and individual ownership, association in the sense of interrelationship, and privacy. Through the centuries, these rights have been the acknowledged objectives of wars and revolutions, of civil disobedience and conscientious objection. They have been upheld, in one form or another, by establishments as diversified as the Roman Senate, the Greek city-state, the British Parliament, and the United States Supreme Court. It is logical that social work should find in them and their accompanying values both the rationale and the governing principles for its disciplined efforts to cope with human needs.

Ownership as Value and Right

It is a major tenet of democracy that the individual has a right to own property, to enjoy it, and to retain or dispose of it at will. This right is "according to nature's law" and, as defined by Aquinas, "is necessary to human life for three reasons" which are as valid today as they were seven hundred years ago. First, ownership is founded on common sense as well as on nature since "every man is more careful to procure what is for himself alone than that which is common to many or to all." This principle is supported by the second reason, that "human affairs are conducted in more orderly fashion if each man is charged with taking care of some particular thing himself." Therefore, Aquinas concludes, "a more peaceful state is ensured to man if each one is contented with his own."[4]

In spite of changing ideas and ideals, these reasons continue to support America's commitment to ownership as value, right, and need—a commitment that is implicit in the Declaration of Independence, explicit in the Bill of Rights, and formally sanctioned in civil rights legislation. Paradoxically, the full significance of the value often becomes most apparent when the right is violated and the needs are vindicated. This fact was demonstrated during the long, hot summer of 1965 when men and women, no longer contented with being deprived of possessions, whether material or psychological, resorted to overt protest—a reaction which, according to the report of the prestigious National Advisory Commission on Civil Disorders, was "firmly rooted in the basic values of American society, seeking not their destruction but their fulfillment."[5]

In theory, ownership and its rewards are protected by the instruments of justice and the traditions of democracy. In practice, they are highly vulnerable. Laws can be broken or poorly enforced; traditions can be honored in the breach rather than in the observance. Such contradictions are aggravated by the dual character of ownership which is, at one and the same time, individual and social. Man can use, fail to use, or misuse his possessions without legitimate interference as long as these actions do not infringe on the rights and values of others. When they do, the body politic has the right and the responsibility through the judicial process to intervene in the interests of the common good. Once again, the dilemma of democracy comes into the foreground and the prerogatives of the one and the many are pitted against each other in the bid for supremacy and sanction.

The balance is difficult to maintain in a competitive society where the desire for material things keeps the production-consumption cycle in motion. Ownership of property, income, or money is a status symbol; it is the hallmark of individual and social security and, most of all, of power. The power struggle, whether among minority groups, union members, industrial giants, or academic institutions, may indicate progress. Unfortunately, it also accounts for much of the imbalance that plagues the experts in fields as widely separated as world trade and human services. The advocates of tariff controls face as difficult a battle as the advocates of social reform, with a single variant. The former are fighting for possession as right and value; the latter are fighting for it as right, value, and need. The added goal complicates the pattern because need is a variable and the means to its satisfaction are controversial. There are no firm criteria for establishing need and no firm statutory procedures to support the efforts to meet it. On the contrary, such efforts are too often determined by the uncertainties of political or social action and the ambivalence of individual or social conscience. There is no stronger confirmation of this fact than the fate of the Family Assistance Plan in 1972.

The pattern of the social services in the United States—from the charity organization movement of the 1870s to the income maintenance programs of the 1970s—has reflected, in principle, the ownership-power concept. Under the early Poor Laws, both in England and the American colonies, the basic criterion of need was destitution in the sense of absolute want. The poor were those who consumed but did not produce. In a society dominated by the work ethic, such persons were consumers not through natural right but by a sense of duty on the part of society, a duty which could be performed or ignored at the discretion of a ranking authority, whether an overseer of the poor, a legislator, or the administrator of a social agency. The poor and the destitute had no right to enjoy possessions, to have money, or to make decisions.

This belief was explicit in the pauper laws of the various states and in the relief in kind which was the modus operandi until the Social Security Act made cash grants mandatory. Even this provision was largely nullified in principle by the freedom of individual states to limit the amount and kind of property an individual could retain and still be eligible for the various categories of income maintenance. Proven need continued to be the deciding factor even when income by right was established by law. Too often, the proof itself was contingent on disposing of possessions which were negligible in terms of monetary value but priceless in terms of human values.

Ownership as Need

The Depression of the 1930s, with its impact on rich and poor alike, confirmed what psychology taught and social work had experienced from the turn of the century—the emotional significance of ownership. This significance does not imply that material possessions are, or ever should be, ends in themselves; the miser and the profligate have equally distorted views of their real worth. It does, however, substantiate the fact that it is natural for man to find through his possessions acceptable means to ends that are his alone. Some men, following the values of a Vincent de Paul or a Francis of Assisi, do this by a kind of dis-possession, by renouncing not the right but its exercise. This is their means to a desired end. But for the common man, to possess property or money or remunerative employment is a right that he cherishes and a need that he strives, with varying degrees of energy and sacrifice, to fulfill. It is, according to Pope Leo XIII, one of the chief points of distinction between man and the animal creation. Deprived of its exercise, he reacts in ways that too often jeopardize the right itself, exaggerate the needs, and contradict the values to which he honestly subscribes.

Two studies, dating back to pre- and post-Depression years, clarify these reactions as they were expressed among the clientele of agencies administering financial assistance. The behavior of human beings deprived of possessions was recognized as a challenge to the knowledge and expertise of social work as a profession.

In a study published in 1929, Grace F. Marcus explored the significance of money, as a form of ownership, to a selected group of dependent families known to the Charity Organization Society of New York. She found that for them, as well as for their independent neighbors, money was more than a symbol of power. It "establishes the measure of family and personal adequacy; it therefore fixes the social status of its possessors. Consequently clients suffer a severe fall in the social scale, in their own eyes and the eyes of their neighbors"[6] when they are deprived of it. The fall brought with it a sense of failure and stigma which, if prolonged, affected negatively every aspect of their lives—mental, spiritual, physical, and environmental. Some expressed their feelings in helplessness; they became as dependent emotionally as they were materially. Others developed a kind of false self-sufficiency marked by blustering demands or hostile tirades. Many, however, maintained a degree of resourcefulness in the face of crisis which is characteristic of the American temperament and drive for independence.

Fifteen years later, in a study sponsored by the Federal Security Agency, the forerunner of the present Social Security Administration, Charlotte Towle explored the same question within the framework of public assistance. She agreed with Marcus that the infinitely complex subject of money has intense emotional significance for those who are deprived. Its absence denotes weakness, frustration, and failure just as its presence is a symbol of adequacy, security, and "even of worth." *Common Human Needs* is based on a review of the case histories of dependent families within the ten-year period after financial assistance was recognized formally as a personal right and a social duty. Towle found that even a program based on right did not prevent, or compensate for, the disruptive effects of prolonged dependency. Mandated programs could supply physical wants but not emotional needs. No matter how humanized, they could not provide the sense of adequacy and self-respect that the normal human being experiences when money or work or property enables him to provide for himself.[7]

These findings are obviously significant for the practice of social work in that they contribute appreciably to a deeper understanding of human reactions to economic dependency. They are equally, although perhaps less obviously, significant for what is revealed about the rights and values associated with ownership. The economically deprived person is unable to exercise his constitutional right to possessions and he responds either positively by fighting for the right or negatively by succumbing to the impairment. Whichever form the behavior takes, the results are a violation of human dignity insofar as they threaten or destroy the self-image and the self-respect which should accompany life in a democratic social order. Thus, social work, as an instrument of society, must understand and treat the denial of ownership as a denial of the rights and values that the profession is designed to uphold and preserve.

Association and Privacy: Twin Rights

It is a paradox of democracy that the system accords equal recognition to the right of reciprocal association and the right of privacy. These constitutionally established rights and the needs to which they give rise find common ground in values that belong to the nature of man as an individual and a social being. It is natural for him to reach for the companionship of other men while, at the same time, he remains separated from them by the cloak of his own identity. He extends himself simultaneously in these two directions because, as a member of the human species, he is like other men and, in his uniqueness, like no other man. He is not an island, neither is he a megalopolis; and so, realistically, he is caught in yet another form of democracy's own dilemma—that is, how to maintain the privacy and sustain the association which are equally essential to his own and society's good. How can he keep the balance between his own world and the world around him and thereby discharge his responsibility to himself and the social order?

In a democracy, the answers to these questions are embodied in a legislative system that reflects the will of the people and in the social institutions to which they subscribe. Laws and the rule of law exist for the equal protection of the many and the one. The former are, in the words of the Athenian Stranger in Plato's "Laws," "partly framed for the sake of good men, in order to instruct them how they may live on friendly terms with one another."[8] The instruction is as necessary in A.D. 1970 as it was in 400 B.C. because, to quote former Chief Justice Warren, "The responsible citizen does not live in isolation. He recognizes that he is part of a community, a state and a nation, and that in playing his part he must act in relation to, and with consideration for, all others."[9] The rule of law protects these same citizens from the violations perpetrated by those who "refuse to be instructed" and for whom judicial procedure is more a necessity than a safeguard. It guarantees the practical application, through orderly measures, of the laws promulgated by men themselves.

Practical application depends for its success on a variety of established institutions—family, church, state —and, since the mid-nineteenth century, on social work as an instrument of the social order. By the mid-twentieth century, according to Gordon Hamilton, this instrument carried "unique responsibilities in the shaping of human events," among them that of mobilizing "the conscience of the community through processes addressed to interpersonal relations." The commitment followed professional recognition that "knowledge of the nature of man, of how his personality functions in the life experience, must be joined with knowledge of society—the development of one is inextricably bound with the improvement of the other." The assumption offered a basis for the emphasis on social functioning as Werner W. Boehm formulated it in his analysis of the nature of social work. The principle had been identified previously in the *Working Definition* formulated by the Commission on Social Work Practice; Boehm clarified its meaning by relating it to social interaction. More recently, Harriett M. Bartlett has extended the concept as a focus for professional practice directed jointly toward individual growth and social improvement. Her emphasis is on the interaction as well as the interrelatedness of the personal and social orders.[10]

If this principle is followed, professional activities will be directed primarily toward maintaining the essential balance between the individual good as exemplified in man's right of privacy and the social good as represented in the right of association. The ongoing process requires a discipline of give and take and a flexibility in dealing with human relationships which social work can exercise because it operates at both ends of the psychosocial event. It is "perhaps, the only profession in which involvement of the whole person within the whole situation is the goal and process."[11] As long ago as 1922, Mary E. Richmond recognized this goal when she defined social casework as those processes which develop personality *"through adjustments consciously effected, individual by individual between men and their social environment* [italics in original]."[12] She found in these processes the essentials of both personal and social development.

Association as Right and Need

Two historic documents on human rights are directly responsible for the absorption into the American tradition of the values of association and privacy. The Declaration of Independence states the premise that is basic to the entire system—namely, the "familiar and immortal" statement of the inalienable rights with which men are endowed by the "laws of nature and of nature's God." Furthermore, it places responsibility for protecting these rights on governments which derive their "just powers from the consent of the governed"—that is, from individuals who are privileged to exercise private judgments and express them through the government of their choice. The Articles of Confederation reaffirmed the "truths," applied them to the democratic order as a "firm league of friendship" which binds the states to assist each other, and assured citizens of "free ingress and egress" to and from any state, the right of extradition, and the right to full reciprocity in judicial proceedings. Privacy and association were thus confirmed for those who accepted and respected man's right to a life of his own and a life with other men.

These pronouncements were formalized in the Constitution and made specific in the Bill of Rights. In the process, the democratic ideal moved out of the realm of abstraction—values and principles—and into that of practical application—rights and needs. Rights were defined and society's responsibility concerning them was given sanction. Needs were recognized, at least implicitly, and became open to consideration and action. The rule of law came into prominence as the champion of human rights and of the values from which they are inseparable. The First Amendment guaranteed the right to association and communication through the normal media of speech, writing, and assembly. The Fourth Amendment established the right to be secure in one's person, house, and effects—that is, in one's privacy.

These seemingly dichotomous rights have, since the late 1930s, "produced a constant flow of judicial business." By the late 1950s, they were "a staple of Supreme Court business" as varied groups "claimed infringements of expression and association"[13] when seeking access to public places with the intent "to change ideas and induce action."[14] The challenges were accelerated in the wake of such tragedies as Birmingham and Watts, the disruption of great universities, and the deliberate interference with civilian and military operations in the industrial complex. These and other less violent happenings brought unprecedented recourse to the rule of law and resulted in direct involvement of the legislative and the judicial branches of government. Within a decade, the former passed, and the latter handed down decisions on, the Civil Rights Act and the Voting Rights Act which, taken together, marked a wholly new stage in the constitutional development of personal and social rights. Both the laws and the decisions struck directly at local barriers to the free exercise of the First Amendment and the Fourteenth Amendment by guaranteeing freedom of association and of franchise in ways not previously defined. Paradoxically, however, the actions generated new challenges to the always precarious balance between the right to be social and the right to be individual.

The reasons for the challenges are inherent in the character of the rights themselves: They are grounded in human nature, are basic to a democratic social order, and enjoy legal protection. In 1958, Justice Harlan, in the case of *NAACP* v. *Alabama,* left no doubt about their character and their place in American life. His statement is categorical and conclusive:

> It is beyond debate that freedom to engage in association for the advancement of beliefs and ideas is an inseparable aspect of the "liberty" assured by the Due Process Clause of the Fourteenth Amendment.[15]

Thus, almost casually, association, as distinct from assembly, became a legal right which the body politic was privileged to enjoy.

So much for the legality of association and the mutual relationships which it fosters. These relationships have been, in one way or another, a focal point of the social services from the early activities of the friendly visitors to the sophisticated approaches of the therapists and the informal techniques of the innovators. Richmond recognized their importance in her step-by-step analysis of the method that began with the first full interview in which the worker was challenged "to establish a human relationship" even at the expense of factual evidence. A few years later, the Milford Conference report suggested "certain norms of human relationship" as guidelines the individual might follow in attempting to organize his normal social activities. The capacity to do this independently and constructively was designated as "self-maintenance," a quality which demonstrated the importance of a "thought-out system of social values" and, inferentially, an appreciation of personal rights.[16]

These early concepts of association within the framework of the social services were followed, in the 1940s, by the more sophisticated interpretations of the diagnostic and functional schools of thought. The former viewed the individual as formed by the interrelationship between his basic needs and his physical and social environment—that is, by his associations. The latter focused on the unique use which he made of these associations, especially as experienced within the formalized structure and services of a social agency. The two points of view, even though fundamentally divergent, recognized association as a fact of life, whether it embraced the entire social environment or was confined to the segment represented in a worker-client, patient-therapist relationship. In either instance, the person is accepted as one among many as well as one alone. He needs others but has a right to remain separated from them.

In 1952, Hamilton interpreted this duality within the framework of professional theory and practice. According to her, "The social work obligation is always based on a commitment to welfare [to human rights and needs] and an abiding belief in positive human relationships." Thus, the central problem of professional practice is "how to bring all the insight of faith and science toward the constructive solution" of any difficulties inherent in these relationships. Hamilton saw two fundamental approaches to this problem: namely, "the protection of human rights and the weaving of rights and responsibilities through social communication[association] into the fabric" of man's relationship with other men. The process calls for "recognition, not only of human needs but of human rights and responsibilities," a recognition which ultimately "becomes incorporated into professional method as values and as techniques."[17]

Hamilton thus brings her analysis back to a value

system which first recognizes mutual rights and needs and then sanctions a service-oriented profession which strives to protect the one and satisfy the other. Accomplishment rests ultimately on a profound understanding of human behavior and a continuously deepening knowledge of the personality "which determines and is determined by its society, as well as on the more familiar and accepted data of political and related science." The specificity of legal rights and the ambiguity of human needs, as the two become one in the individual human being, account for the dilemma that surrounds the values from which they spring (association and privacy) and their impact on man and society.

The *Working Definition* formulated by the Commission on Social Work Practice can be interpreted as an extension of Hamilton's thesis. Beginning with a statement on value, the commission identified certain philosophical concepts as the foundations of professional practice. These concepts included the primacy of the individual in society; the interdependence of individuals and their social responsibility to each other; the commonality of needs and the individuality of persons; and the right to self-realization and the obligation of society to furnish opportunities for its attainment. Recognition of this latter obligation was a key factor in society's sanction of programs designed to meet human needs through professional intervention. Such activities demanded both knowledge of human relationships and skill in facilitating "interaction between the individual and his social environment with a continuing awareness of the reciprocal effects of one upon the other."[18] To maintain balance between the two was the avowed goal of social work.

Boehm associated the underlying values of social

work with those of democracy and defined social work within this context. His definition emphasized reciprocal activity (association) or social interaction as the focus of professional effort and placed any disturbance within this area as a legitimate concern of social work. Whether a given problem involved one's self or others, physical environment, or social roles made no difference since these factors are not separate entities as they affect human beings. They comprise a total interactional field in which the individual plays a variety of roles and, in the playing, demonstrates social functioning. Anything that interferes with this functioning is a responsibility of social work. "To this end, the social worker's activities are directed both to relationships among individuals [association] and to relationships between individuals and the organized social resources of the community."[19]

In his 1962 critique, William E. Gordon elaborated on the worker-in-action concept implicit in the *Working Definition* and in Boehm's interpretation. The idea of social work as action rests basically on functional relationships—that is, on man's purposeful association with other men. The action "is the point in time and space where the social worker's existence can affect the course of events for individuals, groups and communities."[20] These events would not occur unless human beings, by virtue of their natural and constitutional rights, engaged freely and openly in reciprocal activity characterized by an interchange of ideas as well as events. To keep this interchange in balance through disciplined intervention is the goal of social work and an inseparable aspect of the kind of association to which democracy subscribes.

Bartlett has suggested an extension of the principle of social functioning which places an additional emphasis on association as value, right, and need. Her frame of reference embraces two basic concepts: task—that is, "the demands made upon people by various life situations"—and coping—that is, "typical patterns of response and action applicable to many people." The cause-and-effect interchange between these two processes then becomes the focal point of social work, including "the problems, situations and phenomena with which it is primarily concerned." This extends the general idea of interaction which is "further refined and focused on the relation between the coping activity of people and the demands of environment." The refinement serves to differentiate Bartlett's interpretation from its forerunners which "centered on the functioning of individuals or groups, that is, on behavior." Instead, attention is directed "primarily to what goes on *between* [italics in original] people and environment [their interrelatedness] through the exchange between them. This dual focus ties them together. Thus person and situation, people and environment, are encompassed in a single concept, which requires that they be constantly viewed together."[21]

This single concept and its dual component (person and situation) offer, in Bartlett's judgment, a much-needed anchor for social work. The fact that this anchor is grounded in the constitutional right of association and the natural right of interrelatedness adds substance to the judgment. Such grounding allows for the human elements of responsiveness, understanding, and feeling as well as for the legal protection which accompanies recognition and sanction. Within this context, social work can persevere as a specialized activity intended to serve man as an individual and a social being.

The Right of Privacy

The right of privacy is undisputed in a democracy, yet it gained prominence in America only as the country moved from an agricultural to an industrial order.[22] In a somewhat paradoxical fashion, the growth of interest accompanied such disparate events as the abolition of slavery, the rise of cities, and the construction of railroads. By the 1890s, Americans were receptive to the idea that privacy was not only a right but a value worth protecting by law. The idea was synthesized in what was to become a historic document, the work of two young Boston lawyers, Samuel D. Warren and Louis D. Brandeis. "The Right to Privacy," published in the *Harvard Law Review* was essentially a plea for protection against the intrusion of others, with special reference to the press.[23]

The twenty-eight-page article covered three aspects of the question of privacy: the need for a law, the underlying principles, and the limitations. The authors were convinced, both by theory and experience, of the importance of legally protecting the right to be let alone and the right to one's own personality. They contended that certain common law and equity remedies could be expanded to support this argument, such as the law of copyright, which they interpreted as based on the principle of "inviolate personality," not on that of private property. They also attempted to set limits by equating the coverage of the law "with material which would be protected by qualified privilege under the laws of libel and slander." This provision would exempt matters of public and general interest from the personal protection afforded by legislation. The difficulty of defining *public and general* as distinct from *private and specific* soon became evident. Three-quarters of a century later, the experts are still trying to determine, legally, the fine line between the two. The right of privacy, like that of ownership and association, is entangled in the ongoing struggle between individual well-being and the common good.

The article by Warren and Brandeis stimulated new interest in these issues but effective response did not come about until the 1940s and 1950s when efforts to clarify and interpret the legislative role were accelerated. Don R. Pember attributes the movement primarily to the influence of the mass media.[24] Sharpened investigative reporting and rapid dissemination of information resulted in increasingly frequent recourse to the rule of law. The activity was supported in principle in the Preamble to the *Universal Declaration of Human Rights* and made specific in Article 12:

> No one shall be subjected to arbitrary interference with his privacy, family, home or correspondence, nor to attacks upon his honour and reputation. Everyone has the right to the protection of the law against such interference or attacks.[25]

This international consensus was reaffirmed and restated twenty years later in the conclusions of the Nordic Conference on the Right to Privacy, which convened in Stockholm in 1967. In their report, the jurists confirmed the principle that "the right of privacy reflects a fundamental human need which . . . requires the protection of the law." This protection gains importance in "sophisticated and technological society" where infringements tend to increase. However, privacy, as every other human right, can never be wholly free of the limitations "which are necessary to balance the interests of the individual with those of other individuals, groups and the State." The conclusion is that, in fairness to the common good, it is often necessary to grant public authorities certain powers of interference in private matters. But these powers, too, are limited; they "should never be used except for the [specific] purpose for which they were granted." The principle of limitation is thus made applicable to the practice of the law as well as to the theory on which it rests.[26]

The influence of these conclusions is apparent in recent developments in Great Britain and the United States. The former has "no general right of privacy at common law"; the latter has a complexity of laws which vary from state to state. Britain's system of justice depends on individual protection through other laws, especially the law of trespass which covers land, chattels, and person. In the absence of specific legislation, the Nordic Conference recommended action, and in 1970 the Home Secretary appointed a "high powered committee," known as the Younger Committee, to explore the question and:

> to consider whether legislation is needed to give further protection to the individual citizen and to commercial and industrial interests against intrusion into privacy by private persons and organizations, or by companies and to make recommendations.[27]

The Younger Committee report, released in 1972, represents yet another struggle with the old dilemma—

how to balance the public's right to know against the person's right to be let alone. In 1888, an English jurist confirmed this latter right; nearly a century later, the Younger Committee reaffirmed it. An Englishman's house continues to be his castle, even in the absence of drawbridges and castellated roofs. However, since "a general right to privacy could stop the public getting the information . . . which, on occasion, it needs to have," the committee did not recommend the creation of a general right to privacy, "which shall give rise to action in the courts." Instead, by a majority of fourteen to two, the members favored a pragmatic approach aimed at examination of particular abuses of the right through the misuse, for example, of electronic surveillance, credit information, or academic records. This line of action was based on the belief that a broad definition of the right "would have been unduly restrictive of freedom of discussion and dissemination of information which are also vital foundations of a free society."[28] Currently, "there is no reported English decision which determines authoritatively whether or not an independent cause of action in tort for evasion of privacy exists."[29]

In contrast, the Warren-Brandeis study led, eventually, to the development in the United States of an entirely new branch of tort law which covered intangible property—that is, "the products and processes of the mind"—based on a principle, as old as common law itself, which afforded the individual "full protection in person and in property." The authors contended that incorporeal rights issued from corporeal property and that thoughts, sentiments, and emotions were, therefore, included in and should be covered by the right of privacy.[30] This extended concept is reflected in William

L. Prosser's classification of the right of privacy into four separate torts,[31] a classification that was taken up in a 1967 draft designated as the Second Restatement of the Law of Torts. These are: "unreasonable intrusion upon the seclusion of another"; giving unreasonable publicity to his private life; unreasonably placing him in a false light before the public; and appropriating his name or likeness. The operative word, throughout, is *unreasonable.* The restrictive adjective makes intrusion of privacy legally permissible only when supported by principles of justice. The weight of evidence must favor the right and the need of the public to know, over the person's right to withhold.

Today, the right of privacy is legally recognized in thirty-three states and the District of Columbia. Of the remaining seventeen states, four specifically reject the right and the courts have ruled that recognition is a task for the legislature. Another six states maintain a kind of neutrality; they neither recognize nor reject. Five states show no reported cases and apparently have taken no stand. Two states decide reported cases on "other grounds," presumably invoking other laws bearing on individual rights.

The state of California, in its general election in November 1972, placed on the ballot a proposition to amend the state constitution to designate, specifically, privacy as an inalienable right. The arguments in support of the amendment were familiar. "The right of privacy is the right to be let alone" and is increasingly threatened by "the proliferation of government snooping and data collecting." Since *"there are no effective restraints on the information activities of government and business* [italics in original], it is imperative that there be "a legal and enforceable right of privacy for every Californian." The measure was approved by close to a two-to-one vote. Article 1 Section 1 of the California state constitution now reads:

> All people are by nature free and independent, and have certain inalienable rights, among which are those of enjoying and defending life and liberty; and pursuing and obtaining safety, happiness and privacy.[32]

The variation in controls and the aroused concern about the erosion of privacy account for a marked increase in the number of related cases reaching the United States Supreme Court, as well as for some decisions with great and troublesome significance. The cases are far-flung; the decisions are sometimes predictable and other times wholly unexpected. During the last decade, the Supreme Court has heard and handed down decisions on cases involving law enforcement agencies, especially in alleged violations of the Fourth Amendment and the Fourteenth Amendment; freedom of the press versus revelations about private citizens; obscenity and censorship issues; the still-controversial *Miranda* case and the right to be silent; the far-reaching decision in *Loving* v. *Virginia,* which invalidated certain miscegenation statutes; and, more and more frequently, appeals surrounding the use or misuse of computers and electronic surveillance. Norman St. John-Stevas's comment about the English state of mind seems apropos: "Privacy has become almost as fashionable a concept as pollution; the only difference being that most people are as strongly in favor of one as they are passionately against the other."[33]

One group of cases that comes within the search and seizure and the due process provisions deserves mention in the context of the present analysis: the midnight welfare searches of the early 1960s. It became a common practice in many states and in the District of Columbia for agencies administering public assistance programs to make unannounced inspections of the homes of recipients. The declared purpose was to check on eligibility, particularly as it related to the presence or absence of an adult male capable of supporting the family. Sometimes the searches were based on evidence; at other times they were designed as general checks. In either instance, they were conducted without warrants and without previous notification. The practice aroused controversy among the agencies whose rationale was the prevention of fraud; the general public, whose reaction was ambivalent; and staff members who saw it as a violation of professional principles as well as of human rights. The subjects, themselves, had little to say since overt resistance might lead to the termination of a grant.

The issue was eventually settled on constitutional grounds. In an exhaustive and highly technical analysis of the legal implications, Charles A. Reich contended that the practice not only violated both the Fourth Amendment and the Fourteenth Amendment, but it was wholly incompatible with the intent of the Social Security Act as a "guarantee and insurer of the dignity of man."[34] The Department of Health, Education, and Welfare formally prohibited the practice and, in 1967, the Supreme Court of California, in the case of *Parrish* v. *Civil Service Commission,* held that a social worker could not be dismissed "for refusing to take part in a mass midnight raid because the raids violated recipients' rights under the Fourteenth

Amendment." The decision can be looked upon as a double victory; it upheld both professional practice and democratic principle.[35]

The Supreme Court decisions leave unanswered the basic question: What can be done by legal means to reduce invasions of privacy? Henry Kalven, Jr., has enumerated and found wanting a number of existing answers, including the Fourth Amendment, the doctrine of trespass, the so-called common-law copyright, and the more recent attempts to control electronic surveillance and wire-tapping. All of these are technically encompassed by new torts for invasions of the right of privacy which reflect the Warren-Brandeis arguments. Kalven questioned, and admitted that he was among the minority in doing so, the efficacy of the legal approach to real or alleged violations, especially when the press is involved. A person's right to withhold information and the public's right to know are bound to clash, and litigation sometimes hinders rather than facilitates a solution. "The current difficulties with the specific tort of privacy need not mean, however, that the law of the future cannot appropriately find new ways to protect so basic a value."[36]

Kalven does not presume to forecast these ways, but he does anticipate the emergence of countertrends as public opinion becomes more sensitive to the value of privacy and more positive about the right. This reaction could raise "the possibility of locating certain citadels of citizen privacy that could be made inviolate" and which, according to Justice Douglas, might be "sufficiently defined so that the state could not inquire into them."[37] The complexities of such a process are, to borrow a favorite word of the media, mind-boggling. Whether setting limits in this way is admissible in a democracy is a moot question with vast implications. If the answer is affirmative and democratic principles remain inviolate, then the judiciary would be likely to continue to face in the future, as it does in the present, a rising tide of appeals.

The areas involved are bound to be sensitive; population control, both genetic and environmental, private education, and censorship are a few of the highly charged ones. It seems reasonable to assume that even though the Supreme Court had, by the early 1970s, handed down rulings on these issues, the controversy will continue. Present-generation Americans are not easily silenced; for them, argument is a fact of life as well as a constitutional privilege. When the point at issue is the right to give or withhold personal information, the unresolved dilemma about individual and social rights emerges once again, this time in the uniquely human struggle to be let alone.

Privacy and the Social Services

It seems anticlimactic to pursue here the role of privacy in the social services. As value and right, privacy is as germane to the helping process as to democracy. So also are the attendant difficulties. Foremost among these is the protection of the personal revelations which are inevitable whenever one person seeks the help of another, whether physician, lawyer, clinical therapist, or social worker. The sensitive character of such knowledge, both factual and implied, has been recognized since the time of Hippocrates. Even in the casual atmosphere of the

1970s, the physician is expected, as a prelude to practice, to "solemnly swear . . . that whatsoever you shall see or hear of the lives of men which is not fitting to be spoken, you will keep inviolably secret." Likewise, the *Code of Professional Responsibility* to which the lawyer subscribes includes a canon on "the ethical obligation of a lawyer to hold inviolate the confidences and secrets of his client." The *Ethical Standards of Psychologists* include confidentiality as a primary obligation. *The Code of Ethics of the Education Profession* mandates the withholding of confidential information except under special circumstances. The social workers' *Code of Ethics* makes respect for privacy a professional responsibility.[38]

The principle is clear; its implementation in practice is often cloudy, owing, at least in part, to the fact that professional codes offer broad guidelines, not specific directives. They are per se abstract and general; their application to a particular area such as privacy involves decision-making in which the professional person exercises responsibility as to what he should do and, in the process, "takes upon himself a risk." The risk is compounded by the autonomous character of the decision; it represents the "personally responsible, intellectual activity" which Abraham Flexner considered to be "the first mark of a profession."[39] Such autonomy is in the grand tradition of the learned professions and is their legacy to social work. This makes it incumbent on a young, and still controversial, profession to exercise the utmost discretion in regard to privacy.

The task is not easy, either for administrators, who are often bound by legislative or policy regulations not of their own making, or for practitioners who must conform to these regulations. Professional staffs at both levels face repeatedly the ongoing dilemma that is as old as the right of privacy itself—how to protect individual confidences and yet waive that protection when society establishes its right to know. The answer is especially difficult to find in a computerized age where data-processing is routine and data banks can furnish information at the touch of a finger. There is no gainsaying the fact that once the mechanized knowledge is supplied the human subject becomes highly vulnerable.

This vulnerability poses an immediate challenge to social work in the areas of policy and practice. The positions that agencies should take and the controls they can initiate and enforce are questions for the experts in administration and management as well as in professional ethics. The issues are sufficiently crucial to warrant examination within their own frame of reference.

The dilemma which surrounds privacy as a value rooted in human nature, a right protected by the Constitution, and a need such as that which sent Thoreau to the woods and pond of Walden has its counterparts in the related values of possession and association. Democracy guarantees, in principle, the need for and the right to private ownership, and it mandates its protection through the rule of law. Similarly, the need and the right to enjoy companions of one's own choice are legally protected. Realistically, however, these values are threatened, both immediately and in the long view, by conflicting theories and practices bearing on the helping process. The ambivalence that surrounds the strategies of helping —whether the pattern should be that of benefits which presumably insure independence or of services administered in such a way as to preserve dignity—may not be resolved in the foreseeable future. Even if consensus is reached in this area, such fundamental issues as the redistribution of property and the equalization of social status will continue to plague democracy as a system in which "generous, idealistic movements will persist but society will not be radically altered."[40]

It thus becomes incumbent on social work, as an instrument of society, to support these efforts, assuming that they conform to professional beliefs and standards. The responsibility stems both from a commitment to the helping process and from the capabilities of professional personnel. Social workers, as specialists, possess knowledge and skills that can be applied to the solution of social problems as well as to the alleviation of individual needs. They are in a position—whether as educators, administrators, or practitioners—to meet the challenge of protecting values through social activism as well as through personal service. Perhaps this activism reflects most significantly the professional understanding of generic issues as related to special needs. It should mean, according to Kenneth H. McCartney, "the ability to analyze objectively socio-economic problems in terms of whether specific proposals are valid in meeting stated objectives." It should encourage social workers "to continue to develop and advocate—carefully and realistically—programs that will, in time, diminish the difference between what is and what might be."[41]

NOTES

1 Jacques Maritain, "The Rights of Man," in *Man and the State* (Chicago: University of Chicago Press, 1951), p. 97.

2 From "The Lesson for Today," in *The Poetry of Robert Frost,* ed. Edward Connery Lathem. Copyright © 1942 by Robert Frost. Copyright © 1969 by Holt, Rinehart and Winston. Copyright © 1970 by Lesley Frost Ballantine. Reprinted by permission of Holt, Rinehart and Winston, Publishers.

3 Maritain, "The Rights of Man," pp. 101–2.

4 St. Thomas Aquinas, *Summa Theologica* (New York: Benziger, 1947) 2: 1476.

5 *Report of the National Advisory Commission on Civil Disorders* (New York: New York Times Co., 1968), p. 236.

6 Grace F. Marcus, *Some Aspects of Relief in Family Casework* (New York: Charity Organization Society of New York, 1929), pp. 38–40.

7 Charlotte Towle, *Common Human Needs,* Public Assistance Report no. 8 (Washington, D.C.: U.S. Government Printing Office, 1945), pp. 80–94.

---

8 B. Jowett, *The Dialogues of Plato,* "Laws," Book 9 (New York: Random House, 1937), 2: 625.

9 Earl Warren, *A Republic If You Can Keep It* (New York: Quadrangle Books, 1972), p. 167.

10 Gordon Hamilton, "The Role of Social Casework in Social Policy," in *Social Casework in the Fifties,* ed. Cora Kasius (New York: Family Service Association of America, 1962), pp. 28–35; Werner W. Boehm, "The Nature of Social Work," in *Objectives of the Social Work Curriculum of the Future* (New York: Council on Social Work Education, 1959), pp. 47–48; Harriett M. Bartlett, "Toward Clarification and Improvement of Social Work Practice," *Social Work,* 3(April 1958):3–9; and Bartlett, *The Common Base of Social Work Practice* (New York: National Association of Social Workers, 1970), pp. 84–117.

11 Hamilton, "The Role of Social Casework in Social Policy," p. 34.

12 Mary E. Richmond, *What Is Social Case Work?* (New York: Russell Sage Foundation, 1922), p. 98.

13 Gerald Gunther and Noel T. Dowling, *Cases and Materials on Individual Rights in Constitutional Law* (Mineola, N.Y.: The Foundation Press, 1970), p. 467.

14 Ibid., p. 554.

15 Ibid., p. 735.

16 *Social Casework Generic and Specific, A Report of the Milford Conference* (New York: American Association of Social Workers, 1931).

17 Hamilton, "The Role of Social Casework in Social Policy," pp. 29–30.

18 Bartlett, "Toward Clarification and Improvement of Social Work Practice," p. 7.

19 Boehm, "The Nature of Social Work," p. 47.

20 William E. Gordon, "A Critique of the Working Definition," *Social Work*, 7(October 1962):5.

21 Bartlett, *Common Base of Social Work Practice*, pp. 94–99, 116.

22 Don R. Pember, *Privacy and the Press* (Seattle, Wash.: University of Washington Press, 1972), pp. 3–15.

23 Samuel D. Warren and Louis D. Brandeis, "The Right to Privacy," reprinted as an appendix in Adam Carlyle Breckenridge, *The Right to Privacy* (Lincoln, Neb.: University of Nebraska Press, 1970), pp. 133–52.

24 Pember, *Privacy and the Press.*

25 United Nations, Universal Declaration of Human Rights, article 12, final authorized text, 1948; reprinted April 1968.

26 "Privacy and the Law," in *A Report by Justice* (London: Stevens and Sons, Ltd., 1970), appendix B, pp. 45–49.

27 *Report of the Commission on Privacy* (HMSO Cmd 5012), as quoted in Norman St. John-Stevas, "The Pursuit of Privacy," *Illustrated London News*, September 1972.

28 Ibid.

29 "The Present Law in England," in *A Report by Justice*, p. 8.

30 Warren and Brandeis, "The Right to Privacy," pp. 136–40.

31 William L. Prosser, "Privacy," *California Law Review,* 48(August 1960): 389–407.

32 State of California, *Proposed Amendments to Constitution,* General Election November 1972, proposition 11, "Right of Privacy" (Arguments, pp. 26–29; full text, appendix p. 11).

33 St. John-Stevas, "The Pursuit of Privacy."

34 Charles A. Reich, "Midnight Welfare Searches and the Social Security Act," *Yale Law Journal,* 72(June 1963):7

35 Robert J. Levy et al., *Cases and Materials on Social Welfare and the Individual* (Mineola, N.Y.: The Foundation Press, 1971), pp. 321–22.

36 Henry Kalven, Jr., "The Problems of Privacy in the Year 2000," *Daedalus,* 96(Summer 1967):876–82.

37 William O. Douglas, quoted in Kalven, "The Problems of Privacy," p. 881.

38 American Bar Association, Chicago, *Code of Professional Responsibility,* July 1969, Canon 4; "Ethical Standards of Psychologists," *American Psychology,* 18 (January 1963):56–60; Mary J. McCormick, "Professional Codes and the Educational Process," *Journal of Education for Social Work,* 2(Fall 1966):57–65; National Education Association, Committee on Professional Ethics, *The Code of Ethics of the Education Profession,* July 1963; and *Code of Ethics* (New York: National Association of Social Workers, 1969).

39 Abraham Flexner, "Is Social Work a Profession?" in *Proceedings of the National Conference of Charities and Corrections* (Chicago: The Hindmann Company, 1915), pp. 576–90.

40 Robert Morris, "The Place of Social Work in the Human Services," *Social Work,* 19(September 1974):519.

41 Kenneth H. McCartney, "Social Services: Idealism, Power, and Money," *Smith College Studies in Social Work,* 44(November 1973):12–13.

3
The Democracy
of Helping

In recent decades, the enactment of civil rights laws in the United States has marked a new era in the constitutional support of individual liberties. Throughout the 1960s and early 1970s, the thrust of legislative and judicial activities has been to define more precisely the rights of men, women, and children in a democratic society. Corresponding duties, generally speaking, have not been stated *de facto* or defined *de jure*. This omission confirms Gunnar Myrdal's judgment concerning the American creed with its "stress on individual rights and the complete silence on citizens' duties."[1] Duties have been left to individual judgment and the rule of conscience, both of which can be fickle. This absence of objective controls has led to the disparity between ideals and actions which Myrdal has identified with the American scene. He describes the nation as one which "believes in and aspires to something much higher than its plane of actual life."[2] Its citizens do likewise. They subscribe, often enthusiastically, to what ought to be and refuse, with equal enthusiasm, to assume responsibility for changing the *ought* to *must.* For example, the nation and its people deplore poverty, racism, and a host of social ills but too often reject the obligation to take corrective action. This ambiguity, according to Myrdal, leaves America "continuously struggling for its soul."

Helping: The Primacy of the Individual

Perhaps it was out of this struggle that the nation developed a social conscience and expressed it in a method of helping based on the major tenet of democracy, the primacy of the individual. As this method of helping (social work) gained definite form and substance in the days of Mary E. Richmond and her colleagues, the systematic application of the principle became an integral part of practice. In the minds of the pioneers, the operative word was *systematic.* These dedicated men and women were committed to the belief that the helping process must be orderly as well as personal. They saw no conflict between efficiency and sympathy, hence their support of the Charity Organization Society movement, with its emphasis on objectivity and coordinated effort, and of Friendly Visitors, with their "intimate and continuous knowledge of and sympathy with a poor family's joys, sorrows, opinions, feelings and entire outlook on life."[3] The orderliness was necessary because, as Richmond expressed it several times, "we are dealing with human beings, and any lack of efficiency on our part is not merely our loss but theirs." Sympathy was of the essence because dignity and rights are in jeopardy whenever a person needs help to maintain, or regain, control of his own behavior. Richmond thus gave stability and depth to the helping process for many years beyond her own time.

During these years, which coincided roughly with the second quarter of the century, social work as an instrument of helping gained both knowledge and expertise from the behavioral and social sciences and from such diversified fields as law and medicine, physics and mathematics, history and political science. At the same time, its leaders were directly involved in generic issues—freedom, justice, and equality. This involvement was inevitable since they functioned as an integral part of a society committed to the well-being of all of its members, not merely some. When this commitment was strengthened by the Social Security Act in 1935, social work assumed an added function, that of arbiter. It became the conscience which acted in the mutual interests of the common good and individual welfare. The helping process was then viewed as an opportunity to achieve the necessary balance between the rights and obligations of the body politic and those of the persons who comprise it.

The principles remain unchanged in their application to the individual in a changing social order. The individual has the right to the help he needs and the corresponding responsibility to use it for his own and society's good. The social order is obligated to provide such help and has the right to expect that it will be used constructively. The position of the two parties is not always in balance, however. The social obligation is *de jure;* the personal obligation is largely *de facto* and herein lies the basic conflict. In the American culture, personal rights are not merely taken for granted but are defined and sanctioned by the law of the land. Conversely, obligations are seldom mandated. Their fulfillment is likely to depend on individual conscience and on group or community standards, not on legal definition or sanction. They can be honored in the breach rather than in the observance, and society has little redress.

The absence of objective controls over personal obligations is largely unavoidable in a democracy; no law can specifically identify and directly enforce individual sanctions. The midnight searches of the 1960s demonstrated the point. This attempt to impose the obligations surrounding aid to fatherless families was summarily terminated as a violation of constitutional rights and human dignity; democracy would not tolerate the invasion of the former or the threat to the latter. Paradoxically, this very intolerance, supported though it is by democratic principles, jeopardizes those principles since "insofar as man emphasizes rights rather than obligation . . . he defeats democratic ideals and in so doing endangers democracy's very existence."[4]

Charlotte Towle interpreted this mutuality of rights and obligations in an analysis that is valid for all social work, generic and specific. Writing in 1939, she described the philosophy of casework as "essentially a democratic ideology" and its practice as a "sustaining force within an imperfectly realized democracy." As a force, social work represents society's attempt to make up for its imperfections through formalized service provided to persons during times of stress and strain. Its impact is all the greater because, at such times, "in the minds and feelings of the people, the agency is their government—

society itself." To the extent that this reaction prevails, it is vitally important that the primacy of individual rights be reflected throughout the helping process. The person, not the agency or the social worker, must always be the center of activity. In this position he is protected from intrusion, either psychological or operational; he is free to make his own decisions and to be responsible for his own actions. Democracy guarantees this freedom, constitutionally; social work preserves it in an experience that is essentially democratic. In Towle's words, "The autonomy of the individual rather than the autocracy of the agency" becomes the prevailing influence. The person remains free "to realize *his* [italics added] own identity through searching for truths and faiths that serve *his* [italics added] purpose" and affect his behavior both immediately and in the long view.[5]

To be genuinely democratic, however, the individual's searching must embrace responsibilities as well as rights. Social work, as an instrument of society, has an obligation *"for and to* [italics in original] the community as well as *to and for* [italics in original]" its own clientele.[6] In order to meet this obligation, the helping process counts among its objectives the encouragement of the person to develop a greater awareness of his dual role as an individual and as a member of society. In the former, his freedom to exercise his rights is, under normal circumstances, unchallenged; in the latter, it is circumscribed by the rights of others. His obligation to respect these rights is potentially the balancing factor in human association. The principle is axiomatic in a democracy and basic to the practice of social work. Its application is uniquely difficult in both areas since, given the human equation, rights and duties seldom balance. Nevertheless, helping, as a social and an individual responsibility, finds some degree of constancy in the interrelatedness of two fundamental institutions: the democratic structure which defines principles and the professional credo which governs practice.

The Democratic Structure

In his *Adventures of Ideas,* Alfred North Whitehead described modern society as a "coordination of professions," that is, of activities which "are subjected to theoretical analysis, and are modified by theoretical conclusions derived from that analysis . . . It is for this reason that the practice of a profession [including that of helping] cannot be disjoined from its theoretical understanding and *vice versa.*"[7] In other words, the scientific knowledge, generic and specific, which dominates a profession leads, in turn, to the adoption of practices which reflect the knowledge base. These practices then become subject, either before or after the fact, to the governing institutions (the organizations, codes, and advisory units) which the group itself establishes and which ipso facto have legislative or judicial powers analogous to those of a democratic society. Such powers include the freedom to make decisions relative to policy and practice and the authority that gives sanction to those decisions.

The freedom to make decisions accounts for the flexibility which allows, and often encourages, a profession to modify or abandon a course of action on the basis of changing knowledge, both academic and experiential.

The authority indicates the prestige the Western world accords to membership in a profession. Both flexibility and authority are strengthened by their interdependence —flexibility relies on authority and authority licenses flexibility—and by their mutual reliance on the scientific method. The cycle is demonstrated every time the members of a profession act freely and judgmentally on their own recognizance—that is, on their individual or collective reasoning. Communication with peers rather than with outsiders is their pattern. The results may be influenced by physical or psychological factors, but the decisions themselves are based on the objectivity which characterizes political and professional freedom and authority.

According to Talcott Parsons, professional authority represents "a peculiar sociological structure" within the broader structure of democracy. It is based on the superior "technical competence" of the professional person. This expertise and the accompanying "specificity of function"—rather than social status, economic resources, or position in a chain of command—account for the license that society grants to professionals in the crucial area of decision-making.[8] Specialization rather than generalization thus becomes the foundation for a type of authority that is uniquely free and yet "is always limited to a particular field of knowledge and skill."[9] Outside of that field, whatever it may be, the professional is a layman; he shares with the commoner the truism that "everyone is an unskilled laborer to someone else."[10]

Parsons thus establishes the professions as an institutional framework surrounding a constellation of specialized activities which have become "so closely interwoven in the fabric of modern society" that they are essential to its smooth functioning. If this framework is ever seriously impaired, the social order is bound to suffer because "the pursuit and the application of science and liberal learning are predominantly carried out in a professional context."[11] Here, again, the interdependence of the political and the professional is emphasized. The professional context takes form and substance from democratic principles which foster "the social mingling of liberty and compulsion"[12] as these concepts are identified in the Bill of Rights and sanctioned by the rule of law. The same context then offers a foundation for welfare, both in the generic sense of well-being and in the specialized sense of organized or corporate efforts for social betterment of a class or group. The latter meaning is applicable to social work in its dual role as an instrument of society and a channel of service. Insofar as the service reflects the coordination of scientific knowledge and technical competence, it belongs within the combined structure of democracy and the professions.

It would be presumptuous to attempt a review of the democratic system in its cycle of progression and regression over the past nineteen hundred years. It is sufficient to point out that, during the present century, the fundamental principles of justice and charity as the foundation of rights and duties have found their way into programs, both legislative and voluntary, which express the social —if not always the moral—conscience of the Western world. In the course of this penetration, the established teachings have been examined under the microscope of science and applied within the structure of the professions. As a result, they have acquired an aspect of newness that is more apparent than real. Basically, the principles and their expression in practice put the wisdom of the ages into contemporary guidelines for helping man to help himself and his fellowmen. Their substance is the Judeo-Christian culture; their form is the democracy of Plato's *Republic*, "a charming form of government, full of variety and disorder, and dispensing a sort of equality to equals and unequals alike."[13]

Against this background, social work as "a child of the social sciences"[14] and an adult in the complexities of helping, developed its own structure and perfected the techniques that have become its hallmark. In this process, its leaders have reached out to other disciplines for contributions to theory and practice, have tested the materials thus acquired, and have consolidated the whole into programs intended to be "aligned with the struggle for the survival of democracy."[15] Since the life of the democratic system depends on the lives of the people who support it, the programs are focused on human beings in their struggles with the internal and external problems of everyday living. Harriett M. Bartlett identifies this orientation as a "permeating characteristic" of social work as a profession whose aim is to help the person to develop and protect his capacity to function adequately and securely in the social order.[16] The strengths of a realistic helping process are reinforced by the democratic ideals which give direction, measure, and value to the efforts. The cycle completes itself as the structures of democracy and of the profession converge in a unified thrust for the enrichment of life under a government which, it is to be hoped, "shall not perish from the earth."

The Professional Credo

Professional freedom intensifies the personal responsibility which is fundamental to the democratic order and to its institutions. Those who, individually or collectively, enjoy the one must bear the other. They must commit themselves to that self-discipline which John W. Gardner calls the "free man's yoke" and which demands great perseverance on the part of those who, by virtue of their status, are subject to internal rather than external controls. Because these persons are human and, therefore, vulnerable, they need support in this "hard, serious business of self-government."[17] This "serious business" is itself complicated by the co-existence of the independence which the professional cherishes and, in this age of specialization, the interdependence which he can not ignore. The result is ongoing challenge: The liberty that belongs to the one must be kept in balance with the restraints imposed by the other. Perhaps this is the commonsense rationale for the formalized codes of ethics which are traditional to the professions. The codes, "which are designed to state in advance what the sociologically supported behavior" of the membership should be, have become a distinguishing component of professional structure and function.[18]

Wilbert E. Moore describes these codes as "private systems of law" built into the professional structure by its own members.[19] They represent internal consensus on the actions and reactions of the members toward clientele, colleagues, and community. From the practical standpoint, the codes offer guidelines for persons who are equal but not identical and yet must meet, with some degree of unanimity, the demands of a profession and a social order they share in common. To the extent that the demands can be anticipated and provided for within the group, the possibility of individual conflict is reduced. The person finds some degree of security in the judgments of his peers and in the realization that he is not alone; his associates who face the same questions will arrive at substantially the same answers. In the last analysis, however, the codes are no more than directional. In the tradition of democracy, final judgment represents the personally responsible intellectual activity of an individual, not a group, who must exercise great discretion as to what he shall do. To quote Abraham Flexner:

> He [the member of a profession] is not under order; though he is cooperating with others . . . his responsibility is not less complete and not less personal. This quality of responsibility follows from the fact that . . . the thinker takes upon himself a risk.[20]

He can neither abrogate nor delegate the responsibility and the accompanying risk since each is, in essence, a measure of the price of his freedom.

This principle of responsibility originates in the concept of human dignity as the raison d'être for the helping process as well as for the democratic process. The democratic process relies on personal accountability; the helping process relies on professional integrity, ethical codes, and the internal regulative bodies, such as committees on ethical standards. Ernest Greenwood describes these means of enforcement as "case studies in social control."[21] For both processes (the helping and the democratic), the focal point of effort and their primary mandate are the preservation or restoration of the individual's innate worth. The codes of the major helping professions—law, medicine, education, psychology, social work—confirm this mandate in their opening statements.

The *Code of Professional Responsibility* adopted by the American Bar Association is representative of, although more detailed than, the others. The preamble opens with the following statement of principle:

> The continued existence of a free and democratic society depends upon recognition of the concept that justice is based upon the rule of law *grounded in respect for the dignity of the individual* [italics added] and his capacity through reason for enlightened self-government.[22]

The canons that follow are "statements of axiomatic norms, expressing in general terms the standards of professional conduct expected of lawyers in their relationships with the public, with the legal system, and with the legal profession."[23] These canons are augmented by a section on ethical considerations and one on disciplinary rules. The former are "aspirational in character and represent the objectives toward which every member of the profession should strive." The latter are "mandatory in character [and] state the minimum level of conduct below which no lawyer can fall without being subject to disciplinary action." As a unified whole, the three sections offer both direction and control to the extent that they identify the principles and regulate the practices of those who accept the responsibilities which membership in the bar entails. In the last analysis, however, "each lawyer must find within his own conscience the touch-stone against which to test" his fidelity to these principles as they are challenged in everyday practice.

The codes of other helping professions open with briefer, but none the less categorical, statements:

> The avowed objective of the profession of medicine is the common good of mankind.[24]

> We professional educators of the United States of America, affirm our belief in the worth and dignity of man.[25]

> The psychologist believes in the dignity and worth of the individual human being.[26]

> Social work practice is a public trust that requires of its practitioners integrity, compassion, belief in the dignity and worth of human beings . . .[27]

These statements make explicit the premise from which a conclusion about responsibility can be drawn. Its initial presentation in the various codes is followed by a series of statements, or principles, which comprise the body of the documents. These general directives are applicable to the broadest possible spectrum of cases, not to the specifics of a single case. They identify a range of issues, such as knowledge, motivation, and relationships, placed within the total universe of a profession, not within the here-and-now of a particular setting. Generalization serves to emphasize once again the fact that ultimate responsibility for decision-making and consequent action is unilateral; it rests with an individual, not with a group, even of one's peers. The consensus of such a group can ease the burden of a final judgment but it can not make the judgment. This responsibility and all that it entails are the exclusive right and duty of the one who takes the risk upon himself.

The Professional Responsibility

It is unnecessary to elaborate here on the obligations of the professional to those whom he serves. The challenging question of responsibility has been explored in depth and in detail by philosophers, scientists, and practitioners in their efforts to clarify the principles and the dynamics of the helping process. They seem to agree that the mastery of substantive knowledge and technical skills is the primary duty of those who lay claim to professional status. However, this combination alone will not fulfill the professional commitment. The objective knowledge must be accompanied by motivation that is altruistic rather than egoistic and by integrity that inspires confidence and trust. In other words, knowledge must be directed toward the good of the other, and its use must be tempered by sympathy with and understanding of reactions that, whether rational or irrational, positive or negative, are always distinctively human. These are the qualities which, in combination, identify the professional response to personal disturbance.

Scientific knowledge must be accompanied by what Greenwood calls emotional neutrality. Everett C. Hughes describes the attitude as one in which there is "no special interest such as would influence one's action or advice." The professional "may be expected and required to think objectively" about experiences which he realizes are painful irrespective of their origin—physical or psychological, legal or social. But objectivity, with its emphasis on facts, is not enough; it must be complemented by sensitivity to the impact of feeling and emotion. Scientific response to the total problem must be tempered by human response to the segment of it which, at a given time, is affecting an individual human being. The challenge to professional expertise is thus consolidated in the demand for "an appropriate equilibrium between [scientific] detachment and [personal] interest."[28] The specialist must somehow find and hold the delicate balance between the objectivity and the sensitivity that are so vital to the disciplined effort that is the helping process.

This accomplishment depends in large part on the dynamics of motivation. In the tradition of the professions, altruism, which Webster defines as "regard for and devotion to the interests of others," is essentially a response to human dignity. The focus is on recipient rather than donor, and success is evaluated in terms of the benefits that come first to the former and only secondarily to the latter. This does not mean that the professional can or should be oblivious to personal gains. He lives in a competitive society which believes, at least in theory, that the laborer is worthy of his hire. Within the professional context, however, these gains take the form of rewards, both monetary and honorary, which are primarily symbols of achievement rather than payment for services. They are "ends in themselves, not means to some end of individual self-interest."[29] In the vocabulary of technology, they are the feedback from the efforts made for others and can be recycled for further use. This process is set in motion every time the expert uses his knowledge and skill in the interests of someone who needs them. In doing so, he finds satisfaction, not in an enhanced self-image but in the reflection of that image as it is mirrored in the enrichment of another human being.

Because of the demands that altruism makes on those who are committed to it, there is the problem of controlling both the quality and quantity of services. In principle, services should be available whenever and wherever they are needed; in practice, since there are limits to both physical and mental endurance, overexpenditure can be counterproductive. The hazards of giving way to excessive demands are all too frequently demonstrated—for example, by the lawyer who concurrently pleads so many cases that no one of them is adequately prepared, or by the doctor who treats so many patients that no one of them is really known to him, or by the social worker who engages in multitudinous activities at the expense of concentration on practice. Whether such assent to excessive demands occurs out of zeal, which is laudable, or out of self-aggrandizement, which is not, the danger is that these specialists will lose sight of the single obligation that takes precedence over all others—to make intelligent, sensitive, and disciplined use of one's self and one's talents for "the welfare of the individual in relation to the welfare of society [which is] the purpose and test of every program and of a profession's ethical system."[30]

In the interests of that purpose and the test, the professional must be free to limit his services whenever the quality of his performance is threatened. This prerogative of freedom is covered, at least by implication, in the mandates of regulatory agencies and is made clear in ethical codes. Chapter II, section 4 of the *Princi-*

ples of Medical Ethics states, categorically, that the physician may choose whom he will serve. However, once chosen, these persons must receive "a full measure of service and devotion." The *Ethical Standards of Psychologists* calls for maintaining the highest standards of service and competence. The *Code of Ethics* for social workers emphasizes the personal character of the obligation by stating it in the first person singular—"I hold myself responsible for the *quality and extent* [italics added] of the service I perform."[31] It is a fair assumption that these principles, as implemented in practice, reflect professional judgment, not personal feelings. The decision to give or withhold services does not stem from individual likes or dislikes, opinions or attitudes, convenience or ego satisfaction. Rather, it is based on such objective criteria as areas of specialization, availability of technical resources, present and future commitments, and, above all, the effects on another human being. "The ability to say 'no' roundly when 'no' is right"[32] is an important facet of the composite image of one whose motives are altruistic and whose performance represents sound judgment as well as generous impulse.

Integrity, the Indispensable Quality

Knowledge and motivation are indispensable attributes; they are also ineffectual ones unless they are reinforced by integrity, which Webster defines as "a nice sense of allegiance to the standards of one's profession, calling or position." Those who possess integrity are fortified

against the pressures that are the inevitable result of
status; those who lack it are ready victims of their own
weaknesses. There is no need to dwell on the conse-
quences of the distorted judgments and the selfish motives which characterize the violation of integrity. Before
1974 came to a close, and as the nation approached its
bicentennial, Americans were given an object lesson un-
surpassed in their history. Revelations about the total
absence of integrity among persons in high places left the
country struggling, somewhat blindly perhaps, to revive
the fidelity to principle which led the signers of the Declaration of Independence to pledge to each other and, ex
officio, to the body politic, their lives, their fortunes, and
their "sacred honor."

The professional of the 1970s is not called upon to
pledge life and fortune in the literal sense, but sacred
honor permits no exemptions. Commitment to it is incumbent on those who, by virtue of their calling, accept
responsibility for entering into the lives of others with
the intent to bring about change. They must, without
equivocation, demonstrate what is commonly known as
honesty. It is the basis for the confidence the professional
must inspire in others and the foundation of the self-
discipline that justifies his confidence in himself. To the
extent that he is honest, the professional has the right to
ask, and expect, to be trusted. The expectation is based
on the assumption that the client or patient is not a true
judge of the value of or need for the service he receives.
He must, therefore, accept the word of one who, by
virtue of his role and status, claims the exclusive right to
decide and to perform.

Hughes suggests that, in line with this reasoning,
the *caveat emptor* of the marketplace becomes the *credat*

emptor of the professional setting.[33] The belief opens the way for the confidences that invariably surround the account of a personal problem and the confidentiality with which they are accepted. The person is obligated to tell all the secrets which relate to his personal problem; the listener is obligated to protect these secrets from disclosure or exploitation. The interchange represents two sides of a single coin. Ethical codes give specific consideration to the latter (confidentiality) but, unfortunately perhaps, treat the former only by indirection. The whole subject of the extent of the confidences and the vulnerability of a human being as he reveals them is an open one. The obligation to give an honest account of the problem is reasonable enough. The strategic question, and one which has an ethical dimension, bears on what and how much the professional has a right to know in order to be of service. Expediency on the one hand and privacy on the other suggest the dilemma involved in the answer.

There is no doubt that the professional needs, and has a right to, information which is expedient—that is, which indicates a suitable means to accomplish a given end—in this instance, the well-being of another person. The physician can not diagnose unless he has the clinical picture; the lawyer can not solve the case unless he knows the facts, pro and con. Each one has recourse to established criteria in the form of medical classifications or legal statutes against which he can evaluate what he knows and decide, objectively, the adequacy of the information at hand. If there is discrepancy, he is in duty bound to pursue the matter until he is satisfied that the demands of sound judgment are met. The result may be intrusion of privacy; if so, the justification rests on the professional responsibility to master thoroughly and use honestly whatever knowledge, scientific and personal, is essential to the greater good of the one who is served.

In contrast, the psychologist, social worker, or educator must often rely almost exclusively on his own judgment in deciding what he needs to know about those who come to him. Objective criteria for the decision may be limited to generic knowledge about the problem in general and, for those affiliated with an agency, knowledge of the agency's function, policies, and procedures. Beyond such obviously flexible limits, the specialist who works with highly individualized problems enjoys a kind of freedom both stimulating and hazardous. The revelations to which he listens are emotion-charged. Verbalizing is inherently traumatic and the subject matter is intimate. The result is a human interest story as well as a clinical picture, and human curiosity, whether scientific or morbid, is bound to be aroused. Under these circumstances, it becomes imperative that the confident self-discipline of which Gardner speaks take precedence over the self-indulgence that is tempting. Fortified by honesty, the professional who accepts this free man's yoke is as quick to discourage confidences which are unrelated and peripheral, even though interesting, as he is to encourage those which enable him to use his abilities ethically, confidently, and with the expedience born of integrity.

Whether the confidences are extensive or limited, they are always confidential. Charles S. Levy, in his study of codes of ethics, found the principle of confidentiality to be "virtually universal."[34] However, in practice, exceptions are inevitable and the codes justify disclosure under two sets of circumstances: when the law requires it and when professional judgment dictates it. In the former instance, responsibility rests with the judiciary

and options are defined; in the latter, professional judgment is challenged and decision-making is strategic. As
suggested by Flexner, the professional takes the risks that
are the price of autonomy and authority and exercises his
own judgment on questions vital to the well-being of
another person. The responsibility is his alone; the risks
are lessened only by the knowledge, motivation, and
integrity that characterize sound, honest, and unselfish
choice and action.

The codes offer directives applicable both to the
principle and its modifications. The physician may not
reveal the confidences entrusted to him "unless their
revelation is required by the laws of the state" or unless
it is necessary in order to protect the welfare of the
individual or of the community. Legal regulations and
the doctor's own judgment, rather than the strict rules of
confidentiality, may be the determining factors in disclosure. Similarly, the lawyer is obligated "to hold inviolate
the confidences and secrets of his client" but he must
reveal them in response to a court order or on his own
decision in the interests of justice. Likewise, safeguarding
information is a primary responsibility of the psychologist, yet he is justified in sharing it with colleagues or
public authorities "after most careful deliberation and
when there is clear and imminent danger to an individual
or to society." The educator must "withhold confidential
information about a student or his home" except when
"its release serves professional purposes, benefits the student, or is required by law." The social worker is
pledged, in the words of his code, to "respect the
privacy" of those whom he serves and to "use in a responsible manner information gained in professional relationships." His practice is a public trust as well as a
personal service.

These are the guidelines. Their roots are in privacy as value, right, and need. In substance, they represent the professional conscience, individual and social, and their purpose is to protect insofar as possible the dignity which should characterize the helping process. The difficulty is that principles can be, and are, violated. They are subject to defections within the professional structure and to threats from the democratic order. Defections have a moral dimension; they originate in the personal weaknesses of individuals whose fidelity is questionable and whose practical judgment, or conscience, is distorted. The threats, on the other hand, are implicit in the combined strengths and weaknesses of American democracy in action. The First Amendment guarantees freedom of speech and the press; the Fourth Amendment guarantees personal privacy. Each has the power to contradict the other; electronic surveillance and televised jury trials bring new and alarming dimensions to the dilemma surrounding privacy and its invasion.

Within the framework of the professions, these practices have their counterparts in taped interviews, group meetings, and staff consultations. The fact that these techniques can be potential threats to privacy does not mean that they violate either confidences or confidentiality. Realistically, their function is thoroughly positive insofar as they contribute to, rather than impede, the helping process. However, acceptance and use depend basically on conformity with ethical codes. If the conformity is in doubt, the responsibility for making the decision rests primarily with the individual practitioner. He must weigh and attempt to reconcile generic principles, special circumstances, and professional commitments. In doing so, he comes face to face with what Clinton Rossiter designates as the imperative of responsibility, a phenomenon which is equally crucial in the democratic process and the professional orders. Rossiter believes that "in the end, of course, the fate of American democracy rests in the minds and hearts of men rather than in political machinery or social conditions."[35] Similarly, the fate of the helping process rests in the minds and hearts of professionals who are faithful to ethical principles as well as to specialized practices and who are unreservedly dedicated to the well-being of the one and the many whom democracy empowers them to serve.

NOTES

1 Gunnar Myrdal, *An American Dilemma,* 1st paperback ed. (New York: McGraw-Hill Book Company, 1964), 1:16.

2 Ibid., p. 21.

3 Mary E. Richmond, *Friendly Visiting Among the Poor* (New York: Macmillan, 1899), p. 180.

4 Charlotte Towle, "The Individual in Relation to Social Change," in *Helping,* ed. Helen Harris Perlman (Chicago: University of Chicago Press, 1969), p. 217.

5 Ibid., pp. 230, 231, 217.

6 Harry Lurie, "The Responsibilities of a Socially Oriented Profession," in *New Directions in Social Work,* ed. Cora Kasius (New York: Harper and Brothers, 1954), p. 33.

7 Alfred North Whitehead, *Adventures of Ideas* (New York: Macmillan, 1933), p. 64.

8 Talcott Parsons, "The Professions and Social Structure," in *Essays in Sociological Theory,* rev. ed. (Glencoe, Ill.: Free Press of Glencoe, 1954), pp. 34–49.

9 Wilbert E. Moore, *The Professions: Roles and Rules* (New York: Russell Sage Foundation, 1970), p. 238.

10 Paul Valery, "On Intelligence," in *Fairy Tales for Computers* (New York: Eakins Press, 1969), p. 134.

11 Parsons, "The Professions and Social Structure," p. 34.

12 Whitehead, *Adventures of Ideas*, p. 64.

13 B. Jowett, *The Dialogues of Plato*, "The Republic," Book 8 (New York: Random House, 1937), 1: 816.

14 Gordon Hamilton, "The Role of Social Casework in Social Policy," in *Social Casework in the Fifties*, ed. Cora Kasius (New York: Family Service Association of America, 1962), pp. 28–44.

15 Towle, "The Distinctive Function and Attributes of Social Work," in *Helping*, ed. Perlman, p. 235.

16 Harriett M. Bartlett, *The Common Base of Social Work Practice*, (New York: National Association of Social Workers, 1970), p. 127.

17 John W. Gardner, *The Recovery of Confidence* (New York: Pocket Books, 1971), pp. 54–56.

18 Robert K. Merton, *Social Theory and Social Structure*, rev. ed. (New York: Free Press of Glencoe, 1962), p. 378.

19 Moore, *The Professions: Roles and Rules*, p. 116.

20 Abraham Flexner, "Is Social Work a Profession?," in *The Heritage of American Social Work*, ed. Ralph E. Pumphrey and Muriel W. Pumphrey (New York: Columbia University Press, 1961), p. 302.

21 Ernest Greenwood, "Attributes of a Profession," *Social Work,* 2(July 1957):51.

22 American Bar Association, Chicago, *Code of Professional Responsibility,* July 1969, p. 1.

23 Ibid., pp. 1–2.

24 "Principles of Medical Ethics of the American Medical Association," in Edwin F. Healy, *Medical Ethics* (Chicago: Loyola University Press, 1956), p. 402.

25 National Education Association, Committee on Professional Ethics, *The Code of Ethics of the Education Profession,* July 1963.

26 "Ethical Standards of Psychologists," *American Psychology,* 18:(January 1963):56.

27 *Code of Ethics* (New York: National Association of Social Workers, 1969).

28 Everett C. Hughes, "Professions," in *Professions in America,* ed. Kenneth S. Lynn (Boston: Beacon Press, 1965), pp. 1–6.

29 Bernard Barber, "Some Problems in the Sociology of the Professions," in *Professions in America,* ed. Lynn, pp. 17–19.

30 Charlotte Towle, *The Learner in Education for the Professions* (Chicago: University of Chicago Press, 1954), p. 14.

31 *Code of Ethics,* National Association of Social Workers.

32 Mary E. Richmond, "The Training of Charity Workers," in *The Long View,* ed. Joanna C. Colcord and Ruth Z.S. Mann (New York: Russell Sage Foundation, 1930), p. 88.

33 Hughes,"Professions,"in *Professions in America,* ed. Lynn, p. 3.

34 Charles S. Levy, "On the Development of a Code of Ethics," *Social Work,* 19(March 1974):210–13.

35 Clinton Rossiter, "The Democratic Process," in *Goals for Americans: Report of the President's Commission on National Goals* (Englewood Cliffs, N.J.: Prentice-Hall, 1960), p. 75.

4
The Role of
Values in the
Helping Process

In his Preface to *New Knowledge in Human Values,*
Abraham H. Maslow states that the "ultimate disease of
our time is valuelessness." He describes the present century as an "empty period," or interregnum, between
"old value systems that have not worked and new ones
not yet born." Maslow is confident, however, that
"something can be done about it by man's own rational
efforts."[1] Not every one will agree that old values have
failed. For example, John W. Gardner believes that the
*"problem is not to find better values but to be faithful to those
we profess* [italics in original]."[2] But even the skeptics are
likely to agree that the scientific application of knowledge, old and new, to the complex subject of values will
lead to a better understanding of, and stimulate interest
in, their role as stabilizing forces in a democratic social
order.

Actually, there is nothing unique in this activity. The

The major portion of this chapter originally appeared in *Social Casework,* January 1961.

rational exploration of worth and worthwhileness has persisted within the Judeo-Christian culture; Plato and Aristotle, Moses and the prophets, Paul and the Apostles established the background. The pursuit has survived countless threats of disaster, persecution, and even collapse; it seems to be surviving the shock waves of the 1970s. The fact of the matter is that man, either in spite of or because of the frustrations that are his lot, continues to pursue, with a kind of relentless energy, the objectives that appear to him to be desirable. To those objectives that are identified with personal happiness and therefore have particular meaning in terms of his own well-being, he attaches the name *values*.

Even though these values are abstractions and, therefore, can not be looked at, or touched, or listened to, and even though they belong to the world of the spirit rather than that of the flesh, the tendency is to consider them as realities, a word which, both in derivation and definition, connotes substantive or objective existence. This point of view is, perhaps, nowhere more apparent than in the situations that involve the giving and receiving of help. No persons are more sensitive to it than the members of the helping professions—the educators, the lawyers, the medical personnel, the clergy—whose roles are traditional and well defined. At the same time, no persons experience the impact of this reality more directly, and sometimes more dramatically, than the members of the youngest and most flexible of these professions—the social workers, who, irrespective of particular functions or multiple demands, must grasp the human scene and the human person as a unified, integrated, substantive whole.

From this vantage point, the facts and fancies that

make up a given situation, the thoughts and feelings that color it, the words and actions by which it is communicated are, in their composite formation, infused with values. These values must, in turn, be brought into coherent relationship with each other and with experience; that is, the values must be appreciated as reflecting both the frame of reference within which a person acts and the life experiences that befall him. Only then can the helping process complete its cycle of giving and receiving and become stabilized in the capacity and readiness of the individual human being to develop and use his own resources with conscious, well-ordered intent, in the interests of his own happiness.

Isolating Values

The question then arises: Is it possible to isolate, within the professional framework, certain values which, by their very nature, influence the reactions of the person who needs help and the person or persons who respond to that need?

In *The Teaching of Values and Ethics in Social Work Education,* Muriel W. Pumphrey presented an approach to one aspect of this question—how these values occur in the learning process. She offered a summarization, under eight major headings, of the " 'ultimate values' most frequently mentioned in questionnaires, course content, class audits, and professional literature." The formulation was accompanied by the identification of certain "instrumental values," such as "ideas concerning means

to achieve these goals,'' in terms of how such ideas seem
to emerge in class and field instruction. The two sets of
values were then examined, as a unit, in their relationship
to the total learning experience and to the educational
problems which the subject matter poses.[3]

With this report as a starting point, an ad hoc committee at the University of California School of Social
Welfare at Berkeley undertook to explore the subject
further. The approach to the analysis of values was suggested by an aspect of the committee's deliberations—
that is, the identification of categories of values considered intrinsic to the helping process. Four categories
were identified and were designated as: personal worth,
personal autonomy, personal growth and change, and
social experience. These groupings then became the
framework for the exploration of certain defined values,
commonly recognized in the behavioral and social
sciences, in terms of how these values influence the helping process.

As the analysis progressed, it became increasingly
clear that human response to values is the response of the
whole man in the fullness and totality of his person;
within the normal pattern, no part of him is isolated or
cut off from any other part. He acts as a unified being for
whom integrated activity is a desired goal. Moreover, the
values to which he subscribes are part of a single pattern;
they are interlocking and interactive; they can not be
sharply differentiated one from the other. The values that
surround personal worth influence the values that accompany social experience; social experience, in turn, reflects
and augments a person's appreciation of his own identity.

There is nothing essentially new in this concept of
the integrated personality and its characteristic behavior.

Traditional philosophy has always recognized the teaching; ego psychology reinforces and reaffirms it. It is restated here, in oversimplified fashion, for what it indicates about the difficulty of approaching, with any degree of objectivity and precision, the all-embracing subject of values. Systematic classification, no matter what its basis, leaves much to be desired, simply because the resulting categories can never be mutually exclusive; there is too much overlapping of the factors that make up the human equation. In the interests of formalized investigation, however, it seems justifiable to consider the suggested categories under two major divisions: (1) personal worth and personal autonomy, which share common ground in both philosophical and scientific teaching on the nature of man; and (2) personal growth and social experience, which the field of social psychology has unified through its recognition of the dynamics of social interaction. This chapter offers an interpretation of the first of these divisions; in chapter 5, the implications of the second will be explored.

The concept of personal worth needs little elaboration for members of the helping professions; it has, for years, held the key to their approach to persons and problems. Certain values are attached to man simply because he is man; consequently, his sufferings and his deprivations become a responsibility and a challenge. Efforts to discharge the responsibility and meet the challenge have, by and large, found direction and support in systematic theories about the human being and his worth. These theories can be differentiated, for purposes of interpretation, in line with the basic disciplines they reflect; namely, naturalism, humanism, and philosophy insofar as philosophy is distinct from the other two.

Naturalism

The naturalist approaches the subject of values from the vantage point of the physical sciences which, in turn, supply him with working concepts and methodology. The concepts originate in cause and effect relationships; the methodology, in the traditional scientific process. In other words, the naturalist, in formulating basic concepts on which to proceed, works backward. He moves from observable actions to the beliefs, or values, that, presumably, inspire them. Stated another way, the naturalist examines values as facts that appear in overt behavior and can, therefore, be looked at. He then confirms or refutes the soundness of his findings through the use of established scientific method—that is, by applying logic to observed facts. To the naturalist, this process is the origin of values.

Since the total procedure is carried on in a social setting (man does not act in isolation), values are, at one and the same time, "scientific and social virtues." They are "directly derived from the scientific process and from the rules governing a society in which the empirical scientific attitude is predominant." Within the society "nothing . . . is practical, nothing is even reasonable, if it neglects this empirical study." Objectivity and factual verification by the senses become the criteria of reality and, ipso facto, of values.[4]

At the same time, it is human intelligence that makes this procedure possible. The human mind develops the framework and directs the processes that are, in turn, implemented through human actions. These actions then become both subjects and objects for the orderly investigation and discovery which, for the naturalist, lead to the establishment of human values. It seems logical to conclude that this discipline, which places so high a premium on the scientific frame of reference and its implementation, must place a corresponding premium on the person whose activity is, from the naturalistic point of view, the source from which all values spring.

Humanism

The humanist follows a different line of thought and investigation. His focus is on "distinctly human interests or ideals" and on the "totality" of human experience. He shares with the naturalist the belief that values are in some way derived from human action and interaction, but, basically, he gives precedence to those "inner experiences" that involve thought, imagination, and fantasy formation. Feelings and emotions are recognized for the influence they exert on behavior and for their role in the establishment of value systems. In the resulting judgments, the objectivity of the scientific approach is balanced by the sensitivity and penetration that belong to "empathy and intuition." The final interpretation provides room for such ultimate values as love and creativeness, as well as for "self-actualization"—that is, mobilization, in the interests of personality formation, of all traits that are essentially human.[5]

According to Erich Fromm, a leading exponent of the humanistic approach, values are *"rooted in the very conditions of human existence* [italics in original]." They are established by man himself, and out of his knowledge of the human situation he gives them *"objective validity* [italics in original]." This validity exists "only with regard to the existence of man; outside of him there are no values." This system obviously places man in the very center of its framework. By virtue of his existence, he is the creator of values; he becomes their exemplar by virtue of the integrity and individuality of his selfhood. Personal worth assumes a position of highest importance because on it all values depend.[6]

Philosophy

In contrast to, although not entirely separate from, the interpretations of naturalism and humanism stand the teachings of philosophy—teachings so diversified as to make summarization hazardous. However, it is probably safe to say that the philosopher's concept of personal worth, irrespective of his particular credo, can not be separated from his theories about the nature of man. The leading question for him is not "What are values?" but, rather, "What is this person with whose existence and identity values are so universally associated?"

The full answer lies beyond the boundaries of the present discussion. It is possible, here, only to look briefly at two selected systems of philosophy, each of which offers a frame of reference within which the helping professions can appraise the subject of values. In each of these systems—the ontology of Paul Tillich and his followers and the Thomism of the present-day scholastics

—personal autonomy comes into focus as a corollary of personal worth. This is to be expected because it is in this autonomy that man finds it possible to express, whether constructively or destructively, the self-determination and self-direction which he alone among creatures possesses. Moreover, the importance the Western world attaches to this prerogative of autonomy is, in itself, sufficient reason for its inclusion in any consideration of the subject of values.

Ontology

Tillich believes that values are the "ought-to-be" in being; they are rooted in man's essential nature and are derived from his correct image of what he is essentially, in contrast to what he is actually, in his existence. The factor of correctness in regard to this image assumes major importance. If the image is distorted, values will be distorted; if image and values are distorted, knowledge will likewise be distorted since the system identifies knowledge of values with knowledge of being.

The channels of such knowledge are intuition and experience which, in spite of their complementary character, account for the strain that man undergoes as he intuitively sees the contrast between what he is essentially and what he is actually. The intuitive side of knowledge must, therefore, in the interests of balance, be subjected to the continuous criticism of experience, both of the individual and of mankind. Even so, this acquisition of knowledge—of being and of values—is characterized by ongoing tension. Tillich sees no way of overcoming this state of affairs because "one cannot escape the existential risk in the knowing of values." Yet such knowing is a sine qua non, since it is in man and in being that values have their ontological foundation.

Tillich denies, categorically, that values can be derived from existence; on the contrary, they come "from essential structures of being which appear within existence, though in a state of distortion." He illustrates the thesis as follows:

> If we judge the value of a tree, not from the point of view of its wood or shade value for us but from the point of view of its potentialities as a tree for itself, we compare its actual state with an image, an *eidos* or an idea that we have of its essential nature. We call it a poor or sick or mutilated exemplar of what, for instance, a pine tree could be.

Tillich concludes that the way in which this "essence of treehood . . . is attained and tested is identical with the way in which an *objective* [italics in original] value in this realm can be known, namely, the value of the tree for itself." The conclusion is basic to his entire system and suggests an explanation for the conflict that seems to prevail in it between essence and existence.

The explanation of ethical values follows the same pattern. These values are "commands derived from the essential nature of man"; moral law is this nature "appearing as commanding authority." Man himself is, at one and the same time, the "valuating subject" and the "ontological locus"; moral values originate in him and, likewise, in him find their sanction. This line of reasoning serves to confirm, for the ontologist, the conclusion stated earlier: that values, both general and special, are identical with selfhood. In Tillich's words, "They are determined by what man essentially is."[7]

To these scientists and philosophers, values in toto are based on a knowledge of anthropology, on the study of man as a human organism. According to them, a correct concept of man, as drawn from this discipline, is the only one that will lead to a correct knowledge of man's essential goodness, which is the basis of values. Out of this recognition of goodness there seems to come a focal point of general agreement in the various systems; union established through love emerges as an ultimate value. The unifying character of this love is emphasized by Tillich, Fromm, and other authorities in the fields of philosophy, theology, and religion.[8]

In Tillich's view, this love represents the "universal dynamics of life driving toward the reunion of the separated"—that is, the reunion of man "with himself and his essential being." Pitirim A. Sorokin calls it "the unifying element within the human person."[9] Fromm describes it as the "only passion which satisfies man's need to unite himself with the world and to acquire at one and the same time a sense of integrity and individuality." He develops this concept in *The Art of Loving,*[10] in which he describes love as the "answer to the problems of human existence" and, consequently, of human values.

Thomism

In contrast to the single focus of humanist and of ontologist, the approach of the Thomist is three-dimensional: He views man in his essence, in his existence, and in his relationship to his Creator. This is logical thinking in a system that recognizes man as a being who results from the composite union of physical body and spiritual soul, joined as co-principles in a single nature. The nature is composite in itself and is wholly individual in that it is a reality capable of integrating and directing its own forces in its own way. The being who results from this union and possesses this nature is a living, thinking, feeling person, existing in time and place, and capable of loving and being loved. This person is endowed by nature with reason and will, with the capacity to know and to act, to feel and to grow. In addition, he possesses certain super-natural endowments—the grace and the infused virtues of which the theologians speak—and these make possible to him a supernatural, as well as a natural, life—a life with God as well as with man.

It is in this fact of man's life with God, and the accompanying desire to perfect it, that the Thomist finds the starting point for the teaching of values. According to this teaching, values represent the activity of Divine Intelligence; they originate in the attributes of God—in the truth, the goodness, and the beauty which, among other qualities, characterize divinity. This means that such values exist independently of man in his essence and his actuality; they are not dependent on human drives, desires, or decisions. In their operation, however, they do depend on human intelligence and reason; man can know these values and put them into effect, or he can know them and ignore or violate their dictates. In either event, the values, in themselves, constitute the practical foundation of social life, as well as the criteria against which all human activity can be measured.

The foregoing principles hold true both for general

and for special values, for the truths men live by as well as the specific teachings of the moral law. This is the law originating in the mind of God and operating through the mind of man that isolates, clarifies, and makes specific the goodness or badness of human acts—the acts that man performs as a reasonable, responsible creature, aware of his own identity and autonomy. Insofar as such acts conform to the specifications of the law itself, they possess the quality of goodness, the quality that makes them desirable because they contribute to personal happiness.

In performing such acts, man is influenced not only by absolute values which are unchangeable, but by relative values which reflect a particular code, or culture, or society, or habitat. These relative values are, for all practical purposes, the instrumental values, the ideas and actions that are subordinate to certain goals and accomplishments and which, in character, represent the means to an end rather than the end itself. They can, and do, change as goals change; they are directly, or indirectly, related to given settings and particular circumstances; they represent, in the main, the judgments and decisions of reasonable people, faced with practical issues, that call for deliberate action. When these two sets of values— ultimate and instrumental—complement each other, when they operate in unison rather than in conflict, man experiences in his natural and supernatural life the fundamental security that is so important to him. This is the security that the traditional philosophers call certitude, the resting of the mind in the possession of truth.

It remains, then, for the Thomist to examine, in relation to these values, the concept of love which, for him, is fundamental to all values, since it accounts for the

response of body and soul to the object that is agreeable
to either. This love is of two kinds; one springs from the
body, the other from the will. One is sensitive, the other
is rational; both are essential to human nature. If either
were missing, man would belong to either the animal
kingdom or the angelic order; he would not be man. In
possession of the two, however, he is capable of satisfying
the cravings of his body, whether for food, or shelter, or
sexual gratification, and, at the same time, of humanizing
those cravings through the love that springs from the
will. In other words, he is able to control them and keep
them human.

This rational love is expressed either in the love of
desire—that is, in wanting the good for oneself—or in
the love of friendship—that is, in the benevolent love in
which the good is wanted solely for another. This latter
is the love that recognizes the individuality, the personality, the humanity of the one who is loved. In it the loved
one is seen, not as a part of self, but as another self. It is,
in effect, the love that is encompassed by the second great
Commandment.

When this love of friendship transcends the second
and takes on the character of the first great Commandment, when it is expressed primarily for God's sake
rather than for man's, when the "other" is loved, not for
himself alone but as "the image of God on his way back
to God," then the entire act of loving is raised, through
grace and the virtues, from the level of the natural to that
of the supernatural. At this point, love itself becomes the
concrete expression of man's life in God and God's life
in man. In like manner, the values that accompany the
love are no longer sheerly human ones; they are, rather,

the human manifestations of a divine value, the divine love that diffuses itself in human action and interaction.[11]

The Concept of Love

Perhaps no contemporary writer has interpreted this interaction of the human and the divine in the realm of love in more engaging and, at the same time, more profound fashion than C.S. Lewis. His *Allegory of Love* is a classic in its own right; his *The Four Loves* is classic in its simplicity, truth, and timeliness.[12]

Lewis writes with penetration and perspective about love and its values in a way anyone who loves can appreciate. Moreover, he interprets the subject matter in a fashion that should endear him to members of the helping professions. He is scholarly without becoming lost in theory; he is academic without being rigid. As one reviewer commented, the latter book has "the delightful taste of common sense." Within its pages, Lewis presents, according to an ascending scale of values, the four loves of which man is capable. These loves and their concomitant values permeate the human scene, not as stereotypes but as flesh and blood experiences. In these experiences, the person moves from love characterized simply by affection to the deeper love of friendship, then on to *eros* or the love of man and woman for each other until, at long last, he reaches *agape,* or charity, which is the highest love of all—God's love for man and man's God-given capacity to return that love.

The Helping Process

The teachings examined here are, of necessity, selective. Within their limits, however, they embrace a body of knowledge that leads to a better understanding of the helping process. It does so by focusing on man in his relationship with himself and other men. (The Thomist adds a third consideration: his relationship with God.) Thoughtful examination of these relationships brings the key concepts of personal identity and autonomy into the foreground, as these account for man's fundamental desire and capacity to lead his own life and to meet and solve his own problems. Goal-directed behavior and self-help then become characteristics of the well-ordered personality; they represent, within themselves, the values that the balanced, normal person wants to possess and enjoy.

It is the tradition of American social work to respect these values. Edward T. Devine and Mary E. Richmond, to mention only two of the pioneers, led the way when, in a thoroughly practical fashion, they recognized personal worth as the primary reason for giving encouragement and service to people in time of stress. Somewhat later, the Milford Conference gave formal support to the principle of human autonomy when its participants defined the goal of self-help as self-maintenance, "the organization, by the individual himself, of his own normal social activities."[13] Still later, representatives of various disciplines and programs identified the roots of the helping process with the individual's capacity and freedom to be himself, to make his own decisions, and to work out his own problems. In the interests of both personal and social good, such help was to be given with due regard for the rights of others. The value of the common good was not to be jeopardized by the value of self.

During the present century, these principles of helping have been steadily enriched by advances in the behavioral and social sciences and in the methodology of social work. Psychology and psychiatry have penetrated the complexities of human actions and reactions and their meaning for the individual. Scientific sociology has analyzed the sociopolitical and cultural forces which complicate man's life with other men. Social work, in refining diagnostic techniques and approaches to helping, reaches out to these disciplines for whatever contributions they offer. Educators and practitioners interpret what they find and absorb what they can use. This pattern has been followed with a spontaneity sometimes frowned on by the more conservative members of the profession. However, if the efforts do not violate professional standards and the results increase the effectiveness of practice, this rational use of multidisciplinary resources becomes an important asset in the helping process.

The process itself brings to those who engage in it a heightened sense of the significance of values in individual and social life. Since these values are in themselves abstractions, it is logical to assume that the speculative, as well as the practical, sciences will contribute to a better understanding of their role in human affairs. Consequently, philosophy and theology are at long last being explored for what they can tell about man's response to values and his efforts to attain what is for him, the final value: the enduring happiness that is his birthright.

NOTES

1 Abraham H. Maslow, ed., *New Knowledge in Human Values* (New York: Harper & Brothers, 1959), p. vii.

2 John W. Gardner, *The Recovery of Confidence* (New York: Pocket Books, 1971), p. 97.

3 Muriel W. Pumphrey, *The Teaching of Values and Ethics in Social Work Education,* Social Work Curriculum Study (New York: Council on Social Work Education, 1959) 13:37–61.

4 Jacob Bronowski, "The Values of Science," in *New Knowledge in Human Values,* ed. Maslow, pp. 52–64.

5 Walter Weisskopf, "Comment," in *New Knowledge in Human Values,* ed. Maslow, pp. 199–223.

6 Erich Fromm, "Values, Psychology and Human Existence," in *New Knowledge in Human Values,* ed. Maslow, pp. 151–64.

7 Paul Tillich, "Is a Science of Human Values Possible?" in *New Knowledge in Human Values,* ed. Maslow, pp. 189–96.

8 Noteworthy among these persons and their writings are: Martin C. D'Arcy, *Mind and Heart of Love* (New York: Meridian Books, 1956); Anders Nygren, *Agape and Eros* (New York: Macmillan

Co., vol. 1, 1938, vol. 2, 1939); and Denis de Rougemont, *Love in the Western World* (New York: Pantheon Books, 1956).

9 Pitirim A. Sorokin, "The Powers of Creative Unselfish Love," in *New Knowledge in Human Values,* ed. Maslow, pp. 3–12.

10 Erich Fromm, *The Art of Loving* (New York: Harper & Brothers, 1956).

11 For a fuller explanation of Thomistic teaching, see Mary J. McCormick, *Diagnostic Casework in the Thomistic Pattern* (New York: Columbia University Press, 1954).

12 C.S. Lewis, *The Allegory of Love* (New York: Oxford University Press, 1958); and idem, *The Four Loves* (New York: Harcourt, Brace & Co., 1960).

13 *Social Case Work Generic and Specific: An Outline. A Report of the Milford Conference* (New York: American Association of Social Workers, 1929).

5
The Role
of Values in
Social Functioning

In his analysis of the nature of social work, Werner W. Boehm identifies certain of the profession's essential values with those of a democratic society—the values attached to personal identity and personal worth, to the dignity and autonomy of the individual human being. He then identifies other values that are specific on the one hand to the helping process and, on the other, to social functioning. These specific values are implicit in the cycle formed by "society's responsibility for individual welfare and the individual's responsibility for contributing to the common good."

Within this framework, Boehm develops the concept of interrelatedness and examines the place of social work in this complex of human activity. In doing so, he points out that it is the province of social work to view and to serve man, not only in his totality, as do all the helping professions, but more specifically in the various

This chapter originally appeared in *Social Casework*, February 1961.

roles he is called upon to assume in his life with other people. Acceptance of this concept means taking into account human potential and performance within the established structure of society—on a stage that is complete with props and settings. It means viewing man in his dealings with the "people, things, situations, and values" that comprise his milieu. The resulting services, therefore, in both the form of knowledge and of skills, would have as their foci the "patterns, directions, quality and outcomes" of the social relationships which are the specific concern of social work.[1]

Boehm recalls the fact that there was a time when the profession tended to subordinate social factors and their accompanying pressures to the more personalized aspects of behavior. Greater significance was attached to emotional than to environmental components; understanding frustration seemed more important than understanding the situations that followed in its wake. This approach stemmed from the failure to grasp the complementary character of individual and social phenomena and to recognize the importance of merging them into a unified whole. The resulting lack of balance showed itself in the pattern of activity that social work adopted, a pattern that further delayed the integration of those personal reactions and social responses that characterize man's action and interaction.

However, whether through the new knowledge the years have brought or through a deepened understanding of the old, the lines of thought finally converged in the concept of social functioning.[2] This concept places on society the responsibility to do everything possible, within the boundaries of reason and justice, to contribute to balanced social living; it places on the individual the correlative responsibility to make use of these offerings for the good of others as well as of self. The common good and individual fulfillment thereby enjoy a kind of reciprocity which, if maintained, will assure a balanced, two-way flow of giving and receiving. Social work comes into play whenever that flow is threatened—that is, whenever effective functioning is hampered or broken down. Restoration of balance through focus on social relationships then becomes, at one and the same time, the distinguishing characteristic and the definitive goal of professional social service.

If this suggested focus on social relationships is accepted as a professional hallmark, there is ample reason for exploring the values that belong to it. These are the values that the committee at Berkeley placed in the major categories of personal growth and change and of social experience.[3] Their substantive background is dominantly the material of the related behavioral and social sciences; their concrete expression is the core of contemporary social work. They are, in the main, compatible with the values of society as a whole. However, as Boehm indicates, social work values are not necessarily or always "identical at every point with those predominating in society" or, it may be added, in other professions. At any given time, certain values held by social work may represent a departure, radical or mild, from more generally accepted ones. When this dichotomy occurs, interpretation becomes imperative.

It seems obvious that such interpretation, in order to be effective, must be based on knowledge that is reasonably precise. In other words, the values must be identified before they can be explained. Such identification calls for examination, within the social work frame of reference, of those values that the profession identifies with social interaction. Such an examination should embrace substantive content, as well as content related to the behavior of individuals in their social settings. In other words, two levels of abstraction are involved. The one has to do with theories of motivation, adaptation, and interrelatedness in general; the other focuses on the dynamics of behavior, both individual and social. It is at this second level that the examination encounters the specifics of man's reactions to other men—and vice versa—and, at the same time, reveals his response to the values that he holds in common with other men.

Aspects of Social Functioning

For all practical purposes, an exploration of values may be concentrated on three aspects of social functioning—motivation, performance, and goals. These groupings obviously are not mutually exclusive. As component parts of a larger process, they merge and thus can be examined in terms of their interrelationships. The *why* of human behavior, the motivation, marks the starting point; the *how* and the *what* come into being through actual performance; the *where* finds its beginning and its end in the goals that spell accomplishment and satisfaction, whether for the individual or the group or both. Looked at in this fashion, and in toto, social functioning is essentially a response to values, a response that represents man's co-ordinated, directed reactions to those worthwhile commitments that are shared by all the members of a given social system. Once in force, these commitments comprise a framework of rights, duties, and satisfactions that is respected and supported because it contributes to personal and social well-being.

Theoretically, and in terms of rational psychology, the action or movement known as motivation originates in any form of mental operation (imagination, perception, understanding, and so on) that leads to the discovery of an object that is, in and of itself, attractive and desirable. These qualities spring from the inherent worthwhileness of the object in question and from the challenge that it offers to the mind reacting to it. At the same time, the reaction represents an awareness and appreciation of a given stimulus, both in its present and its future potential—what it means to the person here and now and what it promises in the future. During this cycle of activity, both stimulus and response are fluid—that is, they fluctuate and change—and their impact becomes greater or less depending on two conditions. The first condition is the vividness of the stimulus—how real it seems to the person—and the second is the intensity of the response that it evokes—how acutely he wants it. Both vividness and intensity are accounted for, philosophically, in the nature of man, a nature characterized by the ability to know, to feel, and, ultimately, to move in accordance with the rationality of intellect and the sensitivity of emotion.[4]

Such a movement represents the strivings of man in his totality toward goals and values that are uniquely human. The goals themselves represent the objects of man's desire; his performance, as he moves toward them, may be taken as a measure of their worth. Values, on the other hand, are defined, sociologically, at a higher level of abstraction, because they lend direction to performance. They indicate the ways in which man can live beneficially with other men, and they offer standards by which social living can be measured. The full cycle—recognizing the goals, accepting the values, approving the behavior, and moving in accordance with an indicated pattern—thus becomes synonymous with the functioning process. The substantive knowledge that furnishes the background for understanding the process is systematized in the social and behavioral sciences; operating principles take shape and form as social work applies the knowledge, within a specialized framework, to basic human needs. Both the academic and the professional disciplines classify these needs—each according to the human activities with which the particular discipline is associated. These are the activities of body and mind, emotion and spirit, cultural forces and the social order. Separately and in unison the activities of men bear the stamp of motives, goals, and values. In short, they constitute the realities of social functioning.

Interrelatedness and Balance

The importance of both the behavioral and the social sciences in contributing to social work knowledge needs no elaboration. Educators and practitioners alike recognize the contributions that the two disciplines make to substantive knowledge and its professional application. The fact remains, however, that the contents of the two fields have not been accorded equal status in the curricula of schools of social work. Since the early 1920s, material from the behavioral sciences has been incorporated, and justifiably so, into courses in a systematic and purposeful fashion. The same use has not been made of material from the social sciences. The relevant material from sociology has not been presented in the same organized, integrated fashion that has characterized, for example, the theories of individual behavior, personality patterns, and emotional development.

The dichotomy between behavioral and social science content in social work teaching and its implications for future planning was emphasized in various reports of the Social Work Curriculum Study.[5] Examination of courses on growth and behavior, for example, showed that, in the schools furnishing the requested data, content dealing with the individual as an individual was presented in a fashion definitely oriented to the social work process. In contrast, the material relating to environment was "brought in [to course content] without any such structural approach." As a result, it was difficult for the examiners to determine what portion of such environmental material was considered to be essential to a better understanding of individual behavior and developmental patterns at various stages of the life cycle.

At the same time, content bearing on the interaction of individual and environmental forces emerged early in the analysis and was described as "highly significant." The presence and relative clarity of this material led the panel members to conclude that the concept of interrelatedness—that is, of the individual in his social relationships—was taking on new meaning and gaining new recognition in the educational setting. In the light of this discovery, the panel recommended that substantive content from the background sciences be oriented to, and presented in terms of, this concept. The conclusion and the recommendation, taken together, serve to strengthen what Boehm has suggested—that the focus on social relationships is the unifying point around which substantive knowledge should converge.

If future study supports this premise, then background material related to performance, to what man does and how he does it, must be extended to embrace two sets of factors familiar to social workers. One pertains to social roles; the other to change and its accompanying stress. Each makes steady and relentless demands on any person who strives to function satisfactorily in a complex society. In general, the pressure they exert is on adaptability—that is, on the human potential to fit behavior to new uses. More specifically, within the context of social functioning, the human being is expected to fill a variety of roles and to fulfill the corresponding obligations with the expertise of a quick-change artist. Not only must he be many different things to many different people, but this multiple performance is called for even on those occasions when both activities and responsibilities —as each is looked at in its own sphere—seem to conflict. Over and above all this, every human being faces the challenge of change and its accompanying stress. Paradoxically, this change is the only constant factor, insofar as it is always present, in an otherwise mutable world of ideas and ideals, of personal relations and purposeful behavior.

The answer to this dilemma is to be found in the concept of balance, which is continually being explored in the behavioral and social sciences and in professional practice. In each of these settings, one fact is apparent:

Balance, as it applies to the recognized areas of human activity, is accepted as a key element in man's relations with other men. The dynamics of balance are explained by a variety of experts: Walter B. Cannon[6] focuses on homeostasis as the goal of physiological processes; the theories of Kurt Lewin[7] emphasize balance as the goal of psychological processes. Placed somewhere between the two is the ego psychology of Freud and his followers which, in effect, encompasses some of the principles of each as they refer to the emotional component in man's makeup. The ego is viewed as the agent responsible for maintaining an ongoing reconciliation between the various forces that influence both overt and covert behavior; in so doing, it acts as a balance wheel for the whole of mental life.[8]

Sources of Knowledge

Social work has looked to these various disciplines in its search for scientific foundations. The direction of the search is not challenged. The trouble has been that the search has often ended too soon—for example, when a theory of individual behavior was successfully co-ordinated with the behavior of the individuals whom the profession was attempting to serve. It is true that interpretations of individual psychology almost inevitably embrace certain portions of social psychology and to that extent touch on interdisciplinary content. It is equally true, however, that sociology and cultural anthropology have not been pursued, systematically, for what they can tell about man's life with other men and about the dynamics of the behavior that is synonymous with everyday living.

In 1955, Herman D. Stein focused attention on this state of affairs when he examined the need for "an increasing investment [by social work] in the social sciences." In the course of the examination, Stein identified the three main sources from which returns on such an investment could be expected: substantive knowledge, theoretical contributions, and research methods. He found it impossible—and understandably so—to predict the way in which these contributions might eventually be incorporated into the educational pattern. He did find it possible, however, to formulate a threefold objective or goal toward which the consolidated gains, once made, could be directed. He proposed that they be used to instill in the student a social science point of view, to strengthen the intellectual and scientific content of social work teaching, and to give the student "a sound conceptual grounding in theory, practice, and research."[9]

The place of Stein's formulation in the present discussion is obvious. Certainly the social science point of view brings with it a deeper appreciation of values at various levels of abstraction. By the same token, as course content is strengthened, the desirability of such an orientation becomes more apparent and the motives for possessing it are sharpened accordingly. The "conceptual grounding" to which Stein refers should, ipso facto, strengthen professional practice.

In his discussion, Stein makes the thoroughly realistic observation that because social science is "concerned with raising hypothetical questions for theory and research," rather than with answering questions about practice, social workers tend to be "disappointed" in what these disciplines offer. This reaction is aggravated by the fact that the findings are not—like those of the behavioral sciences—directly applicable to people and their problems. On the contrary, they tend to remain in areas of abstraction and speculation, and social workers find them difficult to comprehend. Even the vocabulary seems strange and unintelligible, perhaps because it has not been popularized, either inside or outside educational circles, as has, for example, the vocabulary of psychiatry. Consequently, even the most academically inclined social workers are apt to dismiss the substantive content thus presented as being out of touch with reality because it seems to be out of touch with their own professional frame of reference. Yet even a cursory look at the material serves to illustrate the applicability of the works of, for example, Margaret Mead in one discipline and Talcott Parsons in the other.

Applicability of Anthropology and Psychiatry

In an article dealing with the relationship between anthropology and psychiatry, Mead identifies certain concepts and processes which, in her judgment, the two disciplines enjoy in common.[10] An interesting aspect of this identification, and one that applies with equal validity to social work, is the emphasis that Mead places on the concept of interrelatedness, on the conjoined events and experiences, whether of the individual or the tribe, that form the pattern of social functioning. She points out that both psychiatrist and anthropologist are trained in the recognition of patterns. The former is involved "in the patterns of particular individuals who have woven the threads of their experience into a special idiosyncratic fabric" and the latter in the patterns shared by groups of individuals "who have selected, not over a single lifetime, but over many lifetimes . . . those particular social forms which, fitted together, make a whole" within which it is possible for them to maintain themselves and preserve their culture.

Following the dictates of his training, the psychiatrist hopes for a better understanding of how a given patient is handling himself in the world; the anthropologist wants to know how a given group of people are handling their lives in the world. Within a different, but obviously related frame of reference, the social worker who subscribes to the concept of social functioning wants to know how the individual is getting along with other individuals and how professional services can be most effective in strengthening that association. According to Mead, the intermingling of psychiatric and anthropological data about the pattern of human activity is the first step in bringing the two disciplines together. The extension of this process of intermingling to include social work data could be the first step in bringing this third discipline into union with anthropology. The union with psychiatry has long since been established. In this way, social work might find its point of contact with the cultural component in social functioning, and anthropology might enrich its store of knowledge about man in his social relationships.

Mead makes some further observations about the performance of the specialists in the two fields which her analysis covers. In her judgment, psychiatry and anthropology, for their successful implementation, depend as much on the skill and insight of the practitioner as upon the theoretical framework within which each operates. She says that both rely on the "observation of living persons, talking, walking and acting," and upon the investigator's ability to use disciplined insights into his own behavior as part of the observations he makes. In other words, the method of each is observation that includes the observer. For the psychiatrist, this means the ability both "to observe and to use his own special preoccupations." For the anthropologist, it means following "the intricate trail of his own difficulties of adjusting to, and understanding the behavior of, an alien people" in order to arrive at a pattern very different from his own.

Again, Mead's analysis can be extended to include the social work approach which places emphasis on mutual interest and activity—on the response of the person seeking help and on the counterresponse of the one who gives it. In this process, the particular relationship that marks the association comes into prominence. It is a relationship in which the social worker uses his whole self —his knowledge, skill, sensitivity, and feeling—as consciously as possible in the interests of another person. The effectiveness of that use—and this is the crux of the entire process—depends on giving the other person a chance to use his whole self, whether consciously or unconsciously, as he shares problems and reactions to problems in an atmosphere of interdependence and interrelatedness.

Applicability of Sociology

As an example of the contributions from sociology, the structural theory of Parsons is worth attention since it bears directly on the role of values in social functioning.

In "Authority, Legitimation and Political Action,"[11] Parsons analyzes the interrelationship of what he designates as the functional aspects of social systems—that is, the value aspect, the institutional aspect, and the political aspect. Although he distinguishes among the three as different levels of reference, Parsons sees them as standing in complex but "relatively definite relations to each other." It is around these relations that his analysis centers.

The first, the *value* aspect, has a triple focus. It embraces "the way in which values and other aspects of a common culture are shared by the members" of a given society; how they become at the same time an integral part of the personalities of those members (Parsons uses the word *internalized*) and simultaneously are institutionalized—that is, take on a definite regulatory role. The *institutional* aspect has to do with the way in which these same values "become involved with the more differentiated social structure"—that is, with the portions of the whole which represent categories of action that can be anticipated among members. Such action may be prescribed, permitted, or prohibited for different persons of different status and in varied situations. The important point is that, in the differentiation, values act as normative patterns in a more specific, particularized fashion than prevails at the first level. They now become regulatory in reference to such definite factors as status, role, or sanction, but not to overall structure.

The third aspect, the *political,* is of special interest in terms of its applicability to the social work frame of reference. Parsons points out that this facet of any given society is usually identified with the practical side of social organization. It is concerned with "the way in which the system is organized for . . . effective collective action or 'public' goals." It represents "a concrete system of interacting human individuals, of persons in roles." Parsons designates such a system as a "collectivity"; its successful functioning depends on the organized participation of individuals, on the roles they assume in formulating and implementing common aims and policies. This activity is subject to control by the regulatory function of the institutional level, which, in turn, takes its direction from the values shared by all the members of any given social system.

It seems logical to find, in this analysis of the structure of societies and in the level of abstraction which it represents, a sociological base for the concept of social functioning which Boehm has formulated at another level. The point of contact between the two can be established in Boehm's identification of social work as an organ of society. In interpreting this identification, which is one of his underlying assumptions, he says that social work as a profession "came into being . . . because it meets human needs and aspirations recognized by society. Hence, it assumes some of the socialization and control functions of society."[12] These functions entail a twofold responsibility. One part consists of the obligation to determine the activities or means by which goals are attained and at the same time to keep these activities flexible enough to meet changing situations. The second part of the responsibility embraces the obligation to exercise discipline and control over practice—that is, to establish and maintain standards and sanctions commensurate with the position of social work in the overall social structure.

The role of values, both individual and social, then becomes evident. They are the directive forces that hold the balance between man and society. Basically, they account, on the one hand, for the fact that every person has a right to self-fulfillment and, on the other, for the fact that every society has a right to benefit from this fulfillment. Likewise, they place on every person the obligation to use, constructively, the resources, both personal and social, that are available to him. Conversely, they place on society the obligation to see that essential resources correspond to existing needs and that such resources are available to its members, either through broad measures that are among society's general prerogatives, or through specialized measures that are the assigned prerogatives of social work. The fact of interdependence thus establishes the position of social work in the social structure and, at the same time, reinforces that position by bringing into sharpened focus the values that lend direction and substance to professional effort.

The conceptual framework into which sociology fits these aspects of interaction and interdependence is perhaps best delineated by reference to Parsons's theories on the "grounding of values."[13] In his system, these values, which in a sense constitute ways in which man can live with other men, are grounded in three main directions: existential beliefs, motivational needs, and the social context. His concept of these directions seems to come close to Boehm's concept of social functioning, although formulated at a different level of abstraction. The summarization of Parsons's concept of the grounding of values which follows is made at the risk of oversimplification. It does not go beyond a bare statement of selected content which seems to be directly applicable to the goals and values of social work as they influence social relationships.

The first of these groundings of values, according to Parsons, has to do with their justification and the problems of meaning. This grounding includes the more or less final answers to questions surrounding the all-important issue of why men should live the way they do and, as a part of the process, influence others to do likewise. In substance, these answers transcend empirical knowledge and find their sources in philosophy, theology, and religion.

The second grounding, that of motivational needs, extends to such issues as what man wants and how intensely he wants it. This extension gives rise to a consideration of the integration of values—that is, to the question of how firmly they are entrenched in the total personality and how sharply they are reflected in the way that personality expresses itself. Degree of integration, then, becomes a key point in the process of living up to, or falling short of, professed values. The problems involved bear on the relationship of values to the "balance of gratification and deprivation, of personal fulfilment or frustration" which every individual experiences in his efforts to be faithful to the standards, both personal and social, to which he is committed.

The third grounding is social context—that is, "the

network of rights and obligations in which an individual's value commitments are made." This network comprises, at one and the same time, the setting in which the sharing takes place and the storehouse of the values that are shared. It is the locus of the process which Parsons calls legitimation of social action—that is, the process in which the integrated values that a person subscribes to as his own are linked with the institutionalized patterns that take shape and form as he shares those values with others. This legitimation, with its emphasis on shared or common values, belongs to "a very high level of generality" and, as such, is applicable "to any mode or type of action in the social system."

The process continues at the level of social functioning and in so doing becomes less generalized. As the social system in which it operates takes on definite boundaries—geographical, cultural, or community-centered—values take on an individualized character, and they may be shared less and have less common assent. In any event, there will be internal differences as well as similarities, and both will influence whatever commitments are made. Goals will reflect the here and the now and will show the effects of objective reality, of the situations and experiences that characterize a particular setting.

The flesh and blood relationships or personal involvements will also become a factor, both in the goals toward which activity is directed and in the values that lend direction to it. The resulting action and interaction tend to be relatively specific; they belong not to any group in any situation but to a particular group in a particular situation. The course that is followed then tends to accommodate itself to aims and desires, capacities and resources, that are, to greater or less degree, individualized and specific. In short, social context at this level is bounded by such dimensions as time and place, beliefs and ideals; it bears the marks of individual behavior and established social background.

Throughout this process, values continue to exert their directive influence as human beings maintain their relationships with each other, both as individuals and as members of the varied social groups which, taken together, form society. If, at any point, the interchange is disturbed, if the balance between the give and the take, the needs and the resources, the goals and the values, is upset, then society is faced with the responsibility to restore the balance and reestablish the interchange.

It is at this point that social work, by virtue of its professional assets, takes its place within the social system as a specialized activity intended to serve man as a social being. Its values are the combined values of the individual and of society; its goal is the enhancement of that combination as it contributes to individual well-being and the common good—to the social functioning which is, in effect, response to values and, as such, is the sine qua non of balanced social living.

NOTES

1 Werner W. Boehm, "The Nature of Social Work," in *Objectives of the Social Work Curriculum of the Future* (New York: Council on Social Work Education, 1959), pp. 39–54.

2 Because this chapter was written in 1961, it does not deal with Harriett M. Bartlett's theory of social functioning set forth in *The Common Base of Social Work Practice* (New York: National Association of Social Workers, 1970). See pp. 36, 43–44 for a discussion of Bartlett's formulation.

3 University of California, School of Social Welfare, Berkeley, ad hoc Committee on Values and Ethics, 1960. The writer was a member of this committee.

4 Mary J. McCormick, *Diagnostic Casework in the Thomistic Pattern* (New York: Columbia University Press, 1954), pp. 114–15.

5 Ruth M. Butler, *An Orientation to Knowledge of Human Growth and Behavior in Social Work Education,* Social Work Curriculum Study (New York: Council on Social Work Education, 1959), 6:30–41; and Muriel W. Pumphrey, *The Teaching of Values and Ethics in Social Work Education,* Social Work Curriculum Study (New York: Council on Social Work Education, 1959), 13:79–90.

6 Walter B. Cannon, *The Wisdom of the Body* (New York: W.W. Norton & Co., 1932), pp. 1–26.

7 Kurt Lewin, *A Dynamic Theory of Personality, Selected Papers* (New York: McGraw-Hill Book Company, 1935), pp. 43–65.

8 Calvin S. Hall and Gardner Lindzey, *Theories of Personality* (New York: John Wiley & Sons, 1957), pp. 29–72.

9 Herman D. Stein, "Social Science in Social Work Practice and Education," *Social Casework,* 36(April 1955):147–55.

10 Margaret Mead, "Some Relationships between Social Anthropology and Psychiatry," in *Dynamic Psychiatry,* ed. Franz Alexander (Chicago: University of Chicago Press, 1952), pp. 401–48.

11 Talcott Parsons, "Authority, Legitimation and Political Action," in *Structure and Process in Modern Societies* (New York: Free Press of Glencoe, 1960), pp. 170–98.

12 Boehm, *Objectives of the Social Work Curriculum of the Future,* pp. 41–42.

13 Parsons, "Authority, Legitimation and Political Action," in *Structure and Process in Modern Societies,* pp. 174–82.

6
Economic Dependency and the Social Services

In 1929 Porter R. Lee described social work as "a developing force in a changing world." As such, it possessed the dual characteristics of a cause that is a catalyst of action and of a function that is action. Its objective was likewise twofold: to arouse individual and social conscience about human needs and to perpetuate that arousal through the organized efforts of the community. As Lee saw it, the mainspring of social work was charity, which represented the cause. But he believed that the momentum of that cause would "never carry over adequately to the subsequent task of making its fruits permanent" without an ongoing system of social services, which represented the function. Particularly in a nation which had become industrialized, urbanized, and affluent in less than a century, the transformation of the social order precipitated transformation of the motives, skills, and machinery of these services. Structure, expertise, and support—traditionally flexible, informal, and dependent on personal commitment—became bureaucratic, professional, and community-based.[1]

Lee saw these developments as indicative of a significant change from the individual focus on "ought to help" to a social focus on "ought to give services." During the 1920s, the pattern was stabilized through the establishment or expansion of a variety of programs, both governmental and voluntary. At the federal level, for example, the United States Children's Bureau increased its activities in research, consultation, and demonstration projects. Concurrently, such private foundations as the Commonwealth Fund supported the child guidance clinic movement, with its multidisciplinary approach to parent-child relationships. Specialized agencies, both public and voluntary, extended their functions "above the poverty line" and no longer measured the need for help solely by the yardstick of financial resources. The growth of psychiatry opened the doors to persons whose problems were dominantly emotional rather than economic. The cumulative result was a new frame of reference for those who believed that society must not only have the emotional desire to help but must also want to provide the instruments or the services through which that help becomes effective.

To Lee and his contemporaries, these changes were inevitable, even though in some ways regrettable. Human needs were no longer presented to the sympathy of men, to their sense of justice and humanitarian instincts. Instead, the appeal was to intelligence and a sense of social obligation. Programs were planned and implemented on the basis of factual data which had been gathered, sifted, and interpreted by teams of experts. The resulting activities were supported by taxation or central financing instead of by direct personal contributions. The excitement of a cause gave way to the prosaic routine of a function; intellectual conviction rather than emotional responsiveness was a controlling factor in the total process. Social work as the instrument for providing services became conceptualized as a social institution. Its roots were in a democratic order, its motivation was social responsibility, and its operations were in the hands of the experts.

The concept of social work as a social institution and the values for which it stood were clouded during the 1930s when both the cause and the function gave way to crisis; social work became embroiled in the realities of common human needs. Congress passed, and President Roosevelt signed into law, the most comprehensive and, in the long view, one of the most controversial pieces of social legislation ever conceived. The intent of the Social Security Act was simple enough: to meet present needs and forestall future ones. It recognized the destructive potential of economic dependency and sought to counter it through programs based on right. Social insurance made it possible for the employed person to accumulate in the present a reserve which he had the right to draw on in the future. Public assistance offered temporary help with current problems and the right to use that help without stigma. Each program sought to protect human dignity as value and right; each was committed to the preservation of individual well-being and the common good.

Meeting Economic Need as Cause and Function

In 1945, after a decade of operation under the Social Security Act, the experts were hopeful about these objectives. Charlotte Towle described public assistance laws as "the culmination of a democracy's conviction regarding its responsibility for human welfare" and characterized their administration as work of "decisive importance." The laws themselves defined their own cause and function: the destructive effects of economic deprivation and the importance of countermeasures through "government service based on human rights." Social work, as the activity most intimately concerned with services directed toward individual and social well-being, was thus given "the opportunity to carry forward and to make real the aims of democracy." It could support the cause through the strength of its own convictions and implement the function through its own expertise. Towle warned, however, that these endeavors must reflect an understanding of human behavior as well as of human want. They must demonstrate an awareness of "not merely what we are doing *for* [italics in original] people but what are we doing *to* [italics in original] them" when dealing with the kind of deprivation which threatens human dignity. Protection of that dignity was accepted as the mutual responsibility of social work and the social order.[2]

The responsibility was reflected in, and supported by, the amendments to the Social Security Act in 1956, 1962, and 1965; it lost ground in 1967 and was further jeopardized in the early 1970s. The progression, or regression, is interesting. The 1956 amendments to the Public Assistance Titles provided a significant extension of the purpose of the act to include promotion of "the well-being of the Nation by encouraging the States to place greater emphasis on helping to strengthen family life and helping needy families and individuals attain the maximum economic and personal independence of which they are capable." The terms *self-support* and *self-care* were introduced and the "maximum utilization of other agencies providing similar or related services whether public or private" was encouraged. Federal funds for the training of personnel were made available and states were urged to use them. These developments, among others, opened "new avenues for making public welfare a more constructive instrument in preventing and reducing dependency."[3] At the same time, they placed the onus of leadership on social work and presented a challenge not equalled since the Depression, when it had for the first time exerted major influence during a national crisis.

The future seemed promising in 1960, when Wilbur J. Cohen predicted that, with the programs of the Social Security Act a "part and parcel of the American way of life," social work could look forward to continued and perhaps even more rapid progress in its responsiveness to human needs.[4] The optimism was justified to some extent in the 1962 amendments which specifically recognized the human desire for independence and the consequent importance of helping dependent persons "to become self-supporting, independent and able to care for themselves." In signing the bill, President Kennedy reemphasized its objectives: to stress "services in addition to support, rehabilitation instead of relief, and training for useful work instead of prolonged dependency."[5] The 1965 amendments extended these principles to the medically indigent (Title XIX) in order to help them "attain or retain capability for independence or self-care." Also, in 1965, the Bureau of Public Assistance was renamed the Social and Rehabilitation Service. Leaders in social work had reason to believe that the "ought to give services" concept was, at long last, accepted as a joint responsibility of a democratic order and a helping profession.

The optimism was short-lived. The 1967 amendments were restrictive and in some ways threatening. They reflected the aroused concern of citizens and legislators over the accelerating costs of welfare programs, the increased numbers of recipients, and the repeated allegations of fraud. Welfare "chiselers," unmarried mothers, and the "chronically" dependent became the targets of debate and the focal points of argument and action. There seemed to be a shift of emphasis from saving people to saving money. Unfortunately, the new amendments succeeded in doing neither. Such restrictive measures as ceilings on grants to families with dependent children (AFDC) and mandatory work-incentive and day-care programs might decrease costs in terms of dollars. They might also, and often did, increase the deprivation of those already deprived and, for mothers of young children, threaten the rights and values so clearly stated in the *Children's Charter* and the United Nations *Declaration of the Rights of the Child.*[6]

This was the climate in which President Johnson signed the 1967 amendments into law. In doing so, he criticized Congress for the "severe restrictions" and declared that "the Welfare system today pleases no one . . . [it] is outmoded and in need of major change."[7] This indictment was mild compared with that of the National

Advisory Commission on Civil Disorders which later the same year declared that "the failures of the system alienate the taxpayers who support it, the social workers who administer it and the poor who depend on it."[8] The judgment was prophetic. By 1970, the public was outraged over welfare in principle, social workers were outraged by welfare in practice, legislators were debating substitute plans, and recipients were hostile or apathetic, depending on the presence or absence of leadership within their ranks. This combination of forces brought disquieting changes to social work both as cause and as function. The key concepts, "ought to help" and "ought to give services," were clouded by new ideas about democracy's responsibility toward human need. Government, as a social institution, preempted the giving of material help but was ambivalent about the services which, within the context of traditional social work, were a part of the total process. The "ought to help" was not questioned; the "ought to give services" remained in doubt. Dependency as a social issue became the cause; democracy's treatment of the victims of dependency became the essence of the function.

Economic Dependency as a Cause

Webster defines *cause,* philosophically, as the necessary antecedent of effect and, practically, as an agent that brings something about, a person or thing that is the occasion of action. It is in this latter sense that economic dependency becomes a cause which has challenged the best efforts of man and society, from the lawmakers of the Roman Senate and the Greek city-states to those of the British Parliament and the United States Congress. Yet the phenomenon continues to baffle the experts and the disconcerting question of why remains unanswered. It seems paradoxical that a sophisticated nation should be unable to cope successfully with a problem—no matter how complex and multifaceted—that has captured the attention of every citizen, from the man in the street to the specialist in human affairs.

Explanations or rationalizations range from claims that too much is being done financially for the economically dependent to counterclaims that expenditures far in excess of past and present ones will have to be made before there is appreciable progress. Both theories were tested during the decade from 1964 to 1974 and the results are more confusing than clarifying. On the one hand, for example, public assistance programs generally have reflected the concern of the body politic about excessive spending. The fear of giving seems to be as real as it was a century ago when the Poor Laws and the Puritan ethic combined to restrict help to a minimum. On the other hand, specialized programs in, for example, the Office of Child Development (formerly the Children's Bureau) reflect a pattern of giving influenced by what "ought to be." Basically, however, there is a common focus: the lack of money as a criterion of dependency.

This means that expenditures, whether restricted for fear of negative effects or increased in the hope of positive results, are circumscribed, *de facto* if not *de jure*, by the "subsistence" definition of poverty as a form of dependency. This definition, according to Martin Rein, seeks to describe the condition "objectively [and negatively] as lack of income needed to acquire the minimum necessities of life."[9] The controlling word is *minimum* which, in this context, implies a relative, not an absolute, standard. Warm clothing, for example, is a minimum necessity in some locales and wholly unnecessary in others. A given family or situation may be classified as above the poverty line according to one set of needs and below it according to another. The contradiction will persist until, as Rein points out, poverty is at long last viewed within the context of society as a whole—political, cultural, and social, as well as economic, financial, and individual. The conclusion is in line with Rein's own description of poverty as "not only a lack of income but a lack of the goods and services necessary to support a desired level of well-being."[10]

By substituting *lack of goods and services* for *lack of income* and *level of well-being* for *minimum necessities,* Rein suggests a broadened base for the approach to economic dependency within the structure of democracy. Social policy and its impact on human welfare—rather than money and services and their effect on human need—become primary forces in advancing the cause. Since the early 1960s, one of its instruments has been advocacy, an approach long associated in law and politics with the promotion of an idea or an ideal pertaining to the good of the many or the defense of the few.[11] Advocacy can be exercised formally in the courts or informally in the community; it can be applied to causes as divergent as the energy crisis and the battered child. Once set in motion, its continuing effectiveness depends on such characteristics as dedication, conviction, and zeal. These words have an old-fashioned sound yet they convey the spirit and the meaning that social work, as a channel of service, is looking for as it faces another major challenge in the 1970s —how to meet the human needs accompanying economic dependency without jeopardizing the human rights and values of the dependent person.

Leaders have sought the answers on a variety of fronts, from the activities of paraprofessional and indigenous workers in unstructured programs to the expertise of skilled practitioners in structured agencies. Irrespective of settings or performers, the thrust has been toward the inculcation of feeling and emotion into a helping process characteristically intellectualized and disciplined. Moreover, the same leaders have urged that priority be given to the social rather than the individualized aspects of dependency—to cause rather than to case. This, in itself, presents a major challenge. It calls upon social agencies to extend their services beyond functions that are specifically defined and, when necessary, to adopt methods that are spontaneous rather than studied. In short, policies, programs, and techniques have to be flexible enough to allow administrators and practitioners to "create strategies of helping and to adapt structures that will conform to the realities of people in trouble rather than to the demands of professional convenience or tradition."[12] Only then can dependency become a cause and advocacy a function of the social services as a joint instrument of democracy and social work.

Unfortunately, the enabling legislation that guides the income maintenance programs does not permit this kind of flexibility. Within its frame of reference, dependency is measured in terms of the presence or absence of essential economic resources such as money and the commodities that money can buy. It is not evaluated against

the effect of continuing deprivation on personal and social well-being, although this is where Towle placed it in
Common Human Needs. Instead of extending to the
broader issues of policy and the long-range implications
of dependency in a democracy, goods and services are
limited by statute to those that bear on proven financial
need. This condition is defined through the so-called
budget approach—that is, the "cost of purchasing a fixed
amount of commodities needed for a socially acceptable
standard of living."[13]

In calculating these costs, the federal government
relies on the single item of food as the unit of measure-
ment. Budgets are adapted to the price of food which
may or may not fluctuate in proportion to the prices of
other goods and services. State and local governments
tend to follow the cost formula but maintain considerable
autonomy in their definitions of such criteria as essential
resources and socially acceptable standards. They can
establish their own regulatory policies and procedures,
such as, for example, California's "workfare" require-
ment and New York City's incredible system for comput-
erizing the entire welfare process. Provisions such as
these lead to wide variations in grants to individuals and
families. For example, in July 1973, the average monthly
payment to a family with dependent children (AFDC) in
the State of New York was $81.32 per recipient and
$286.22 per family. In Mississippi, the average was
$14.48 per recipient and $52.49 per family. During the
same month, grants to the aged averaged $158.31 in
Wisconsin, in contrast to $50.33 in New Hampshire.[14]
Such extremes are inevitable in a system that approaches
the problem from case to cause but that somehow fails to
reach the latter. The figures tell a great deal about the

impact of value judgments, as well as cost analyses, on the way in which affluent America views the economically dependent segment of the population.

Social Services as a Function

Lee's "ought to give services" concept is implicit in the Social Security Act and explicit in the Public Assistance Titles. Nevertheless, it was challenged in practice by the 1967 amendments, and by 1970 the role of social services in the income maintenance programs changed drastically. The federal government took the position that individualized, noneconomic help should be separated completely from financial assistance, because the objectives of the two functions were entirely different. The rationale was that unified operation led to confusion about their relatedness, hampered their implementation, and limited the freedom of recipients in seeking, selecting, and accepting services "without coercion," either real or implied. The major objective was improved administration in both areas. With this objective in mind, in 1970 the Social and Rehabilitation Service strongly urged the states to follow the plan "in the best interests of consumers, taxpayers and welfare agencies."[15]

In attempting to comply with these recommendations, states faced the problem of co-ordinating two independent yet interdependent programs carried on by staff members having different orientations and responsibilities. Workers who handled eligibility were mandated to screen applicants and determine, individually, both the legal right to and the amount of the grant. The entire process was directed by the cost formula and followed the budget approach; final decisions were based on established criteria and could be defended objectively. In contrast, social workers had to cope with subjective needs which could not be reduced to their component parts, given monetary equivalency, or included in a welfare budget. Recognition of their essential character depended on such human variables as professional skills and administrative policies. At best, response came by indirection and on a case-by-case basis. Their defense, in the event of challenge, rested not on social evidence (as Mary E. Richmond saw it) but on recognition of society's commitment to the principles of democracy and the consequent obligation to recognize subjective as well as objective human needs.

What long-range effects this plan might have had on the "ought to give services" concept became an academic question within two years. Early in 1973, the adult maintenance programs were transferred (effective January 1974) from the state welfare departments to the Social Security Administration. Basic grants to the aged, blind, and disabled were subsidized primarily by the federal government and treated as insurance benefits, even though proven need remained the major criterion for eligibility. States were required to supplement the basic allotment, in line with their existing budgetary standards, but only one service from a specified list was mandated —for example, housekeeping service or attendant care. All other activities became optional; state and local agencies could maintain or eliminate services at their own discretion. There is no doubt that the new regulations strike a decisive, perhaps crippling, blow at the role of social services and social work in public welfare. Under such a policy as this, neither one remains an integral and vital part of the total process of meeting human needs.

Meanwhile, state welfare departments retained responsibility for families with dependent children (Title IV), but new federal regulations sharply curtailed the "services in addition to support" principle emphasized in the 1965 amendments. Under the 1973 revisions, only three services were mandated—family planning, foster care, and protective services for children. All others including day care, which had enjoyed some degree of priority, became optional with state and local agencies. Even if provided, day care was in fact restricted inasmuch as it was identified with employment or training for employment. The mother who engaged in either activity could no longer rely on the supplementary resources (health, housing, referral, counseling) which formerly were an integral part of the AFDC program. Although not ruled out by law, these services were bound to be substantially restricted, both in policy and practice, when they were not supported by federal subsidies. The "ought to give services" principle was again threatened, this time for a specified group of women and children.

On the positive side, payment of money benefits, unencumbered by services, reflects an optimistic outlook. It assumes that an individual may have a problem without being one and that economic dependency is not necessarily accompanied by personal inadequacy. On the negative side, money alone may offer dubious comfort to those who are too young or old or handicapped or uninformed to convert it, on their own initiative, into the goods and services they urgently need. For these people, the system may fall short of its objectives unless it is reinforced by complementary services which not only give practical help but also inspire the hope and preserve the dignity that are the hallmarks of the democratic order. In the interest of the "general Welfare" which the Founding Fathers recognized, a firm line of communication will have to be established between needs that engender the "ought to help" and the services that are their counterpart.

Realistically, there was a political factor in these limitations on services. Under the General Revenue Sharing Bill, Congress allocated $2.5 billion for public social services. When added to funds available from other sources, the cumulative total sounded astronomical. Figures for any given month—for example, July 1973—are indicative of the whole. During that month expenditures for all types of public assistance, including medical and emergency, totaled nearly $1.7 billion for 14.7 million persons. Nearly three-fourths of the recipients were families with dependent children.[16] Perhaps, on a per capita basis, and as an indicator of humanitarian responsiveness, the amounts were miserly rather than generous. But to public officials, sensitive to the mood of the taxpayers, they were threatening. Unfortunately, the body politic was disillusioned with the system and, by association, unsympathetic to its victims. A newspaper columnist described the popular attitude: "It [welfare] automatically conjures up not a friendly, indulgent image of helpless children, cripples, and beleaguered mothers, but a repellent cartoon of a big lazy oaf who prefers handouts to an honest day's work."[17] This image of welfare recipients, combined with monetary costs and negative attitudes, made the entire system highly vulnerable.

The confusion, if not outright distortion, seems to

be shared by those among the policy-makers who are skeptical about the essential character of social services and their effectiveness in the public welfare system. Sharon Bishop, writing from the vantage point of management, cites lack of substantial proof on these matters as a complicating factor in planning and administration. She contends that it has not been demonstrated to everyone's satisfaction that the recipients of welfare grants or benefits need services; nor is there evidence that services, when offered, are "fully effective for solving individual and social problems." Granted that universal agreement and full effectiveness are unattainable goals, there is validity in Bishop's argument that present findings are unsatisfactory. She makes a plea for scientific studies and, at the same time, recognizes the technical difficulties in this kind of research.[18] Both design and methodology, no matter how carefully executed, are always vulnerable and findings, no matter how convincing, are inevitably challenged. However, the practical importance of such research is obvious; the efficacy, and perhaps the life, of many programs depend on it.

Income Maintenance and Social Services

There is a related question which also warrants exploration: the function of the social services in systems of income maintenance. During the Depression of the 1930s, the answer seemed clear enough—economic dependency in itself generated the need for services. The two were, for all practical purposes, inseparable. This assumption followed the residual conception of social welfare, that "social welfare institutions come into play only when the normal structures of supply, the family and the market, break down."[19] When this breakdown occurs, the institutions are resorted to as temporary measures which can be eliminated if, or when, the normal pattern of life in a democracy is restored. The principle was given form and substance in the Public Assistance Title and the Social Insurance Title of the original Social Security Act. The categorical programs were society's response to immediate needs; the insurances offered protection against the needs of the future. The assumption was that as more wage earners were covered by insurance benefits (income by right), fewer persons would require assistance grants (income by sufferance). In the meantime, the function of the social services was primarily that of alleviating or reducing human needs through the case-to-cause approach.

This concept of service prevailed for twenty-five years after the act was passed, in spite of numerous amendments intended to broaden the coverage. Then came the unprecedented changes of the 1960s when the attention of the public and of the experts was focused on social services as elements of social policy, not as accidentals related to specific needs. The catalytic forces are too familiar to warrant elaboration here. They found expression in activities that, whether acceptable or controversial, were destined to have widespread impact. These included, among others, the implementation of civil rights legislation, the passage of the Economic Opportunity Act, the commitment to advocacy, and the causes sponsored by such groups as the Welfare Rights Organization. The thrust of these combined movements was to reverse the case-to-cause approach and attack (the word is used advisedly) human needs via cause-to-case. Welfare services were to have their own identity as first-line functions of the contemporary social order.

Before this change could become an accomplished fact, however, services had to be developed, not as delayed expressions of social conscience but as instruments of social policy. Their focus would be social need as a normal human problem affecting society as a whole, not merely those segments for whom economic dependency sharpens the impact. The objective would be prevention on a universalized basis, rather than individual cure. The decision to use or ignore services would be personal and independent of external circumstances such as proven need. In this socialized—using the word in its academic rather than political context—approach to human needs, society assumes responsibility, not only for "people who have been hurt" but also for creating "conditions in which people . . . will not in fact be hurt."[20] The principle is as old as the democratic way of life. For the United States, it was affirmed in the Bill of Rights; for the nations of the world, it was reaffirmed in the *Universal Declaration of Human Rights*. The words of the latter document substantiate both the goal and the challenge: "Everyone, as a member of society, has the right to social security," not as the concept is defined in particular laws or statutes but as it is mandated in those rights and values which are "indispensable for his dignity and the free development of his personality."[21]

The logical move in this direction seemed to be a system of direct money payments, based on statutory right, that would supplement income and, at the same time, leave persons free to work out their own means of coping with whatever discrepancies exist between needs and the capacity to satisfy them. Such a plan would do away with the welfare approach by substituting payments based on a negative income tax formula—for example, as income decreases payments increase, and vice versa. The benefits would extend to the working poor, in the interest of prevention, and to the dependent poor, in the interest of alleviation. Daniel P. Moynihan described the approach as the quintessence of simplicity. People were to be given money and left to their own devices. The hope was that they would find in these provisions enough constancy and security to counterbalance the variables in life that are so threatening. The proposal was neither unique nor untried except in the United States, which has the dubious distinction of being the only industrial democracy in the world without some form of guaranteed income.

The congressional struggles over the Family Assistance Plan are too familiar to warrant recapitulation here. Twice passed by the House only to meet defeat in the Senate, it was allowed to die in committee because, to quote Moynihan, "too many people, from opposite points of view, wanted it dead." The forces at work, pro and con, included such powerful ones as party politics, business and professional interests, community action, and, dominating all others, the attitude of an American public "schooled in the work ethic and the fear of encouraging dependency." So, whether for better or for worse, welfare reform was once again in limbo. Moynihan claims that keeping it in the foreground of the social conscience requires "greater competence and more political courage than the American political system was quite able to summon. But it almost did. And it might yet."[22]

The next major attempt at federal action came in

October 1973 with the introduction into the Senate of the Social Services Amendments of 1973. The bill was designed "to rescue the Social Services programs from regressive regulations" mandated by the Department of Health, Education, and Welfare in September and scheduled to become effective in November 1973. In general, these regulations tightened the existing restrictions on services to families at or below the maximum welfare level by extending from three to six months the period for the redetermination of eligibility. The ruling had the effect of setting excessively low income standards for eligibility for services among potential recipients and tended to negate previous attempts to help marginal families maintain some degree of independence.[23] On the other hand, the proposed amendments provided for greater flexibility in meeting the needs of the working, as well as the dependent, poor. The bill received noteworthy support from public officials, governmental agencies, and private organizations but was not acted on by the Ninety-third Congress.

One year later a new bill was introduced concurrently in the Senate and in the House which would govern the federal-state social services programs. This bill was the joint effort of a social services coalition, representatives of both houses of Congress, and officials of the Department of Health, Education, and Welfare. Among its major provisions was continuation of the $2.5 billion federal commitment for welfare services which, with full state participation, would provide $3.3 billion annually "in services such as child care, protective services for children, treatment for alcoholism and drug addiction, and special help for the elderly, handicapped and others with special needs." The bill also proposed broad federal guidelines under which the states would have primary responsibility for service programs, with eligibility based on income rather than on "welfare relatedness"—that is, qualifying as a former or potential recipient.[24] It received the unanimous endorsement of those who worked on it and who were convinced that it would give federal and state agencies greater freedom to concentrate on getting services to the people.

The optimism may have been justified; certainly the spirit of those who expressed it was laudable. The fact remains, however, that the 1973 and 1974 proposals, once enacted, would perpetuate in principle, if not necessarily in practice, the welfare system which originated in the Social Security Act. The "benefits" of the former and the "supplemental security income" of the latter are updated versions of the public assistance provisions of the 1930s. Proven need, even though more realistically defined, continues to be the basis for helping and the burden of proof continues to rest with the victims of economic dependency, whether the condition results from their own or society's failure. Perhaps in the wake of the controversy aroused by the Family Assistance Plan, this reversal to an established pattern seemed expedient; it is nonetheless self-defeating. Help which embraces monetary payments and social services will alleviate dependency on a pro tem basis. It will not bring the dependent person into the mainstream of independent living in a competitive social order. This realignment can occur only when inadequate help is replaced by adequate income which can be exchanged, in a responsible fashion, for the goods and services that democracy offers.

Two proposals publicized in late 1974—one emanating from the Department of Health, Education, and

Welfare and the other from the Subcommittee on Fiscal Policy of the Joint Economic Committee—bring renewed hope that this replacement may become a reality. The sponsors urge that "the nation's major welfare programs be replaced with a $21.6 billion 'case transfer' plan patterned after the negative income tax" and administered through the tax system. The new plan, designated as the Income Supplement Program, would eliminate the present system of unrelated welfare programs and "transfer by check and through one office, cash subsidies from Washington to eligible individuals and families." All citizens with incomes below a so-called break-even level— that is, "the total sum of a family's personal tax exemptions and its allowable standard deductions"—would be eligible. Under this system "the federal government would recognize for the first time that no prescription of government service programs is likely to lift the bulk of the nation's low income population out of its economic straits." The alternative seems to be to "turn to a cash plan that will offer what poor people are most in need of —money."[25]

It is only realistic to assume that an Income Supplement Program will be as controversial as was a Family Assistance Plan, and for many of the same reasons. In addition, the timing may be unfortunate. In 1975, the proposal will have to compete for attention with such complicated issues as inflation and recession, rising unemployment and rising prices, an energy crisis, and an unbalanced consumption-production cycle. On the positive side, however, it will have the support of the experts, political and professional, and of those citizens who agree that radical change is needed to wipe out inequities and end the nightmare of administering current programs and that waiting can only make matters worse. The choice between the obsolete and the innovative has become imperative. It must be made without further delay even though

> . . . we all may be inclined to wait
> And follow some development of state,
> Or see what comes of science and invention,
> There is a limit to our time extension.[26]

The limit seems to have been reached but the development of state has not yet materialized. Meanwhile, science and invention probe the mysteries of outer space more effectively than the realities of economic dependency.

The Impact on Rights and Values

Among the values emanating from the concept of human dignity, that of personal security has always received priority in the American system of democracy. The Bill of Rights recognized it and subsequent legislation in such areas as education, health, and public safety has confirmed the importance of guaranteeing and protecting "the right of the people to be secure." In the present social order, this security is, for the average person, contingent on possession of the tangible assets of property, income, and capital. Unfortunately, these do not co-exist with economic dependency. On the contrary, property, real and personal, is limited to the essentials of food, clothing, and shelter; income is fixed according to a common denominator of budgetary needs; capital, as a commodity of free exchange, is not available. The effects of the deprivations are predictable. In the absence of material things which belong to him, man loses his sense of belonging; in the absence of independent income, he loses his freedom of choice; and in the absence of capital, he loses his sense of adequacy and, perhaps, of personal worth.

These absences are intensified in a competitive society by the fact that possession, especially of money, is looked upon as a criterion of successful living and a mark of personal adequacy. For these and other reasons, Towle advocated in 1945 what America is still struggling to attain in 1975: unrestricted money payments to the economically disadvantaged and social services for those whose needs extend beyond the economic. The "ought to help" and the "ought to give services" are two sides of a single coin; the effectiveness of each is reduced by separation. This fact alone bears out Towle's conclusion that unless and until programs representing both sides *"are made available to man as his inalienable right to survival, he is doomed to continue . . . [to be] anxiously dependent on others, insecure, and unfree to move courageously into full assumption of adult responsibilities* [italics in original]."[27] Since these responsibilities are among the values implicit in the Constitution and the rights made specific in the amendments, programs to guarantee their security are mandatory in a democracy. As such programs are initiated, the nation and its people face a challenge in which time is of the essence and action must become the order of the day.

NOTES

1 Porter R. Lee, "Social Work: Cause and Function," in *Readings in Social Casework, 1920–1938*, ed. Fern Lowry (New York: Columbia University Press, 1939), pp. 22–37.

2 Charlotte Towle, *Common Human Needs*, Federal Security Agency Public Assistance Report no. 8 (Washington, D.C.: U.S. Government Printing Office, 1945), pp. vii–viii, 1.

3 Eveline M. Burns, "New Horizons in Social Security," *Social Work*, 2 (April 1957):3–7.

4 Wilbur J. Cohen, "The First Twenty-five Years of the Social Security Act," in *Social Work Year Book* (New York: National Association of Social Workers, 1960), pp. 49–62.

5 Quoted in Arthur E. Fink et al., *The Field of Social Work*, 5th ed. (New York: Holt, Rinehart and Winston, 1968), p. 142.

6 White House Conference 1930, *The Children's Charter* (New York: The Century Co., 1931); and United Nations General Assembly, *Declaration of the Rights of the Child*, reprinted in *Teaching Materials on the Welfare of Children* (New York: Council on Social Work Education, 1969), pp. 3–4.

7 Quoted in Fink et al., *Field of Social Work*, p. 147.

8 *Report of the National Advisory Commission on Civil Disorders* (New York: New York Times Co., 1968), p. 457.

9 Martin Rein, *Social Policy: Issues of Choice and Change* (New York: Random House, 1970), p. 448.

10 Ibid., p. 425.

11 Ellen Manser, ed., *Family Advocacy: A Manual for Action* (New York: Family Service Association of America, 1973).

12 Maurice F. Connery, "Changing Services for Changing Clients," in *Changing Services for Changing Clients* (New York: National Association of Social Workers, 1969), p. 31.

13 *The President's Commission on Income Maintenance Programs* (Washington, D.C.: U.S. Government Printing Office, 1970), pp. 10, 28.

14 Department of Health, Education, and Welfare, Social and Rehabilitation Service, *Public Assistance Statistics July 1973* (Washington, D.C.: U.S. Government Printing Office, November 1973), Introductory Statement and tables 4 and 7.

15 Department of Health, Education, and Welfare, Social and Rehabilitation Service, *The Separation of Services from the Determination of Eligibility for Assistance Payments. A Guide for State Agencies* (Washington, D.C.: U.S. Government Printing Office, 1970), pp. 1–3.

16 *Public Assistance Statistics July 1973.*

17 Clayton Fritchey, "A Political View of the Welfare Rolls," *San Francisco Chronicle,* September 10, 1971.

18 Sharon Bishop, "One Way to Assess Needs," *The Social and Rehabilitation Record,* 1 (December-January 1973–74):19–22.

19 Harold L. Wilensky and Charles N. Lebeaux, *Industrial Society and Social Welfare* (New York: Russell Sage Foundation, 1958), pp. 138–39.

20 John S. Morgan, "The Changing Demand for Social Service," in *Changing Services for Changing Clients,* pp. 1–21.

21 United Nations, *Universal Declaration of Human Rights,* article 22, final authorized text, 1948; reprinted April 1968.

22 Daniel P. Moynihan, "Annals of Politics. Income by Right—III," *The New Yorker,* January 27, 1973, p. 81.

23 "Mondale Introduces Social Services Bill," *NASW News,* 18(October 1973):3.

24 "New Social Services Bill Introduced," *NASW News,* 19(November 1974):1.

25 John K. Iglehart, "Welfare Report/HEW Wants Welfare Programs Replaced by Negative Income Tax," *National Journal Reports,* 6(October 19, 1974):1559–66.

26 From "The Lesson for Today" in *The Poetry of Robert Frost,* ed. Edward Connery Lathem. Copyright 1942 by Robert Frost. Copyright © 1969 by Holt, Rinehart and Winston, Inc. Copyright © 1970 by Lesley Frost Ballantine. Reprinted by permission of Holt, Rinehart and Winston, Publishers.

27 Towle, *Common Human Needs,* pp. 49, 56, 57.

7
Professional Responsibility and the Professional Image

When, toward the end of the nineteenth century, the pioneers in American social work committed themselves to programs that required formal organization and to services that necessitated trained personnel, they established ipso facto an alliance with the helping professions. During the early twentieth century, the alliance became identification; social work was referred to as a profession. At the same time, those engaged in social work experienced increasing concern—perhaps even anxiety— about their identity and about the new role they were to assume. How did this role compare with the well-defined ones of those long involved in service to human beings —the educators, lawyers, medical personnel, and clergymen, whose titles were self-explanatory and whose images relatively stereotyped? How could social workers, whose titles and concomitant images ranged from investigator to paid agent and from friendly visitor to case-

This chapter originally appeared in *Social Casework,* December 1966.

worker, find a place in this hierarchy of established professions?

Influence of Related Fields

The answer to these questions seemed to evolve during World War I. Social workers emerged from that period of crisis with a new clientele, a new image, and a new awareness of professional self. This development led to an additional duty for social work: to provide service for persons whose problems were dominantly individual and emotional rather than social and environmental. The helping process thereby became the cause and the effect of a revolutionary union with the behavioral sciences and with medicine—dynamic psychology, which was contributing to the understanding of human beings, and psychiatry, which was only then crystallizing its identity and formulating its approach to the diagnosis and treatment of emotional ills.

The readiness of social workers to follow the dictates of psychology and psychiatry is too well known to warrant elaboration. More important, in terms of the future, was the eventual acceptance of a body of knowledge destined to reinforce the scientific base. In this process, the significant, but nonetheless amateur, interpretations of the early years gave way to the objectivity of twentieth-century thinking.

It was during these formative years that interest in "profession as an honorific symbol" became a controlling factor in social work and in its projected educational programs. This symbol, according to Howard S. Becker, "represents consensus in the society about what certain kinds of work groups *ought* [italics in original] to be like."[1] Present-day society uses it in evaluating occupations and in measuring their moral worth. The symbol thus becomes a criterion of behavior insofar as it embraces ideal characteristics that are valued by those who claim professional status. Becker sees in it "the image of the profession and the professional as occupying an esteemed position in the society . . . [and] entitled to an important voice in community affairs." In the public mind this position of esteem, as Becker points out, is associated with a "monopoly of some esoteric and difficult body of knowledge," which consists "of abstract principles arrived at by scientific research and logical analysis."[2] Such knowledge is considered to be necessary for the continuing functioning of society. It can not be used routinely, but must be applied judiciously on a selective basis. This combination of substantive content and the skill to use it has, traditionally, been counted among the attributes of the professions. Social work came, at long last, to a reliance on both in the shaping of its image.

In the light of such an image, Abraham Flexner, in 1915, raised the question that has persisted for more than fifty years: Is social work a profession?[3] Flexner's answer was inconclusive, and the desire to find a more definitive one has continued to plague those who pursue the subject in a society where professional identification has rapidly become a major determinant of role and status. It is a fact that in the United States today personal and social relationships are vitally influenced by affiliation with one's peers. Each professional association furnishes leadership, establishes media of communication, sets standards and sanctions, delineates values, and directs the formulation of ethical codes. It becomes, in a sense, the superego of its members. It is no surprise, therefore, that social work has consistently sought for itself the attainment of a degree of prestige commensurate with the image of a profession.

Initial Organizational Steps

Formalized efforts to establish standards date back to 1898, when the Charity Organization Society of New York initiated a summer training course. By 1904 this course had developed into a one-year program within the New York School of Philanthropy. Its aim, according to Mary E. Richmond, was "to give our professional charity workers better habits of thought and higher ideals."[4] Within two decades, similar programs were launched in a number of cities, including Chicago, which had its pioneer School of Civics and Philanthropy.[5] By 1919, seventeen educational institutions offered some kind of specialized preparation. Moreover, these institutions were sufficiently conscious of their purpose and identity to form a professional organization, the forerunner of the present Council on Social Work Education.

The high point in educational progress during the first two decades of the present century was certainly the publication of Richmond's *Social Diagnosis* in 1917.[6] Educators and practitioners alike were given—in a book that reflected fifteen years of thought and experience—the first formulation of the point of view and method of social casework. The book synthesized the contributions of many disciplines and brought them into focus within a developing discipline that was becoming standardized in a professional way.

Meanwhile, efforts to further delineate the professional image were exerted along many fronts. In 1921, the first constitution of the American Association of Social Workers was written. Its statement of purpose declares that members of the organization, "acting together, shall endeavor through investigation and conference to develop professional standards in social work."[7] Two years later, the Experimental Draft of a Code of Ethics for Social Case Workers was prepared by the Charity Organization Society of New York and presented for discussion at the national conference. Each of the thirty-seven sections was accompanied by examples demonstrating its application to practice. Although the code was not adopted at that time, it is a prototype of the one that was adopted almost forty years later.

Against this background, the Milford Conference convened in 1923. Its report, published in 1929, was described at the time as a high point in the development of the profession. In the report, conference members did not attempt to analyze the professional aspects of social work, but they did identify the areas in which social casework is distinguished from other professional services. One of these distinguishing marks was the "increasing ability to deal with the human being's capacity for self-maintenance"[8]—that is, for organizing his own normal social activities and thereby freeing himself from the need for professional services. Specialized knowledge and skill were recognized as essential elements in this development. Two years later, Edith Abbott made her own unique contribution in a collection of addresses and papers prepared while she was engaged in organizing a new professional school. Her writings were interspersed with references to the "great profession to which we are dedicated."[9] Ten years later, Esther Lucile Brown concluded that social work had "progressed far in the direction of professional status."[10]

Changes in Society and New Challenges

These judgments that social work had made noticeable progress were especially significant in view of the fact that the programs of the 1930s, established first by statutes and later by federal law, might well have acted as deterrents. Fortunately, such was not the case, because the essentials of principles and practice were by that time defined—both informally and formally in the proposed code of ethics—and because professionally oriented social workers were called upon by governmental agencies to participate actively in the new programs. Through their participation, social workers did much to solidify the professional character of services that were, in line with the intent of the Social Security Act, to be administered "by humans for humans."

The war and the postwar crises of the 1940s brought new challenges to the professional character of social work, which had by that time defined its principles, refined its methods, and sharpened its focus. The primary concern had become the welfare of the individual for his own sake and for that of society as a whole. Consequently, the progress, in theory and in practice, was due in large part to the conscious application of democratic principles and to a deepened understanding of human behavior. Activities were centered on man's relationship with himself and with all the elements of his milieu. The human person and the human scene constituted a substantive whole. Professional service was becoming stabilized around the capacity and readiness of the individual to develop and use his own resources in the interests of his own, and society's, well-being.

Progress of this kind made it imperative that social work and social workers keep pace with their own ambitions by examining, as Charlotte Towle suggests, the "demands implicit in a profession in general and specifically in social work."[11] Towle's presentation at the 1948 Annual Meeting of the American Association of Schools of Social Work was focused on the emotional element in professional education. Her analysis has equal validity when it is applied to the image that education was attempting to create.

According to Towle, the components of the image include a field of service established to serve the common good; a philosophy calling for action that conforms to an established ethical system; the knowledge and skill essential to competent practice; and a unique identity "to which other professions can contribute but for which they cannot substitute." Her contention is that social work stands or falls as a profession insofar as its practitioners make these characteristics come alive.[12] They can do so by developing a truly social conscience—one that will make it possible to subordinate the professional self to a larger identity. When this goal is achieved, the practitioner should be able to work within limits and yet remain creative and free.

Development of Professional Education

Convictions and aspirations such as those expressed by Towle brought social work into prominence both academically and in the implementation of services. The achievements during the 1940s are too numerous to be listed, but the important fact is that they culminated in the full-scale study of education for social work that was one of the first undertakings of the newly formed National Council on Social Work Education.

The Hollis-Taylor report was published in 1951. Although its authors gave recognition to the progress that had been made and the image that was in the making, they were not willing to accord full professional status to social work. They did, however, express the conviction that although the profession had not yet realized its own strength,

> with the increasing responsibilities placed on social work by society, with an impelling grass-roots movement within the profession toward unity, and with a strong leadership pressing for scientific study and evaluation, the profession seem[ed] destined to come into the full use of its powers at an accelerating rate.[13]

There is, perhaps, no better proof of that acceleration than Towle's masterful work, *The Learner in Education for the Professions,* published in 1954. Very early in her analysis, Towle expressed the belief that

> a profession, like an individual, has come of age when it has developed capacity for interdependent relationships, notable qualities of which are readiness to give

> and take without anxiety and without need to domi-
> nate or to suffer loss of identity.[14]

She then proceeded to show how social work strives to perfect this capacity and, at the same time, demonstrate realistically the security of thought and action that is the unmistakable mark of professional performance.

Three years later, Ernest Greenwood identified five distinguishing attributes of a profession, applied them to social work, and thereby outlined the professional image toward which social work aspires. One of these attributes is possession of a regulatory code that offers a starting point for consideration of the composite of professional responsibility and its image—that is, the responsible person extending a specialized service to another person.[15]

Greenwood points out that every profession has a built-in code that compels ethical behavior on the part of its members. This code possesses formal and informal components. A written statement that sometimes carries statutory force, to which a person subscribes when he enters into practice, constitutes the formal part. The informal part is unwritten; it represents the spirit rather than the letter of the law. The formal part derives from systematic thought and objective judgments; the informal part, from various factors, such as emotion and feeling, custom and convention. These complementary parts supply the professional person with a set of criteria and a sense of direction in fulfilling his professional responsibility. The specifics of this responsibility may vary; its essentials are always uniform. In 1960 the governing principles were formalized in the social workers' *Code of Ethics.*[16]

The Individual and Society

Traditionally, social workers have tended to focus on the psychological and material needs of man as an individual rather than a social being. The person, not the community, was for many years the primary object of professional concern. This emphasis probably came about because casework, with its particularized approach, is a long-accepted and familiar form of social work. But new insights and new experiences brought fresh attitudes about man and his community, attitudes shaped by the fact that in modern society neither can function in isolation. Interdependency and interrelatedness were recognized as essential to the well-being of the many and the one. Placed in juxtaposition rather than hierarchical arrangement, each was given some degree of responsibility for the other.

Once this position was established, it highlighted a basic and perpetual dilemma: the potential dichotomy between the best interests of the individual and the well-being of the community. What benefits one may penalize the other, and the social worker is faced with the task of somehow maintaining a balance. In reality, the dilemma confronts fields other than social work. Any profession functioning in modern society, according to Alfred North Whitehead, is faced with the responsibility of making certain that individual rights are safeguarded while a "sense of community" is maintained.[17]

Writing on the same subject, Henry M. Wriston comments that although the principle is easy to state, "its application requires a continuous exercise of judgment and will." This demand results directly from the fact that in a democratic social order and in a world so inter-dependent and so disturbed, "there is perpetual tension between the particular and the general, between individual whims and social necessities."[18] Relief of this tension is brought about through compromise measures that place certain compulsions upon the individual to add to the general welfare as well as to his own. Wriston cites such homely and familiar examples as taxes, vaccinations, and school attendance—all of which have the purpose of developing the individual and protecting society. He concludes that "each is defensible when it does not inhibit essential free choices and when non-performance would involve danger, needless cost, or disadvantage to others."[19]

Governments can exercise this compulsion with precision and in accordance with established routines; social work can do so only with a minimum of regularization and sanction. Its activities (except in authoritarian agencies) have neither statutory force nor legal backing; its personnel does not have the security that comes with the licensing or certification that is meaningful to the general public.[20] Those who engage in social work—and this is a factor of some import—can not rely on a legal definition of malpractice as protection against the unscrupulous within their ranks. Neither can they find prestige in a definite, recognizable image that identifies them with a specialized function, as is true with the physician, lawyer, or clergyman.

Social workers have never experienced—and perhaps never will—this monopoly of service and image. The traditions of the past and the demands of the present seem to dictate that their activity, focused as it is on man's personal and social welfare, precludes this degree of specificity and control. It must remain discretionary rather than mandatory. Their image identifies not a particular function but an ongoing process, the strength of which lies in the fact that it can be accommodated to a volatile human scene.

The Means for Fulfilling the Professional Role

The breadth and flexibility do not imply, however, that social workers have no established means of fulfilling their obligations as professional personnel. On the contrary, they possess a consistent and effective medium in the helping process, the particular combination of knowledge, skill, and resources that has characterized American social work from the earliest days. The origin and orientation of the process are to be found in man himself, in his inherent capacity and constitutional right to direct his life in accordance with his own best interests and with due regard for his fellow man. For all practical purposes, this process is implemented through the professional relationship and professional intervention. Much has been written on the former; less, specifically, on the latter. Perhaps this is so because once relationship is established, it becomes the medium for the kind of intervention that permits one person to share, with impunity and respect, in the life experiences of another.

There is no need to dwell on the place of relationship in social work. Gordon Hamilton once wrote that the handling of relationship "is what characteristically gives the professional quality to any social service."[21] It is de facto germane to the helping process. Its specific character is determined by the focus—whether person, group, or community. Its universal character, as reflected in the demands that it makes on professional personnel, is constant. Such demands can be delineated through an examination of three closely interrelated aspects: the involvement of the worker; the needs of the clientele, whether one person or a group; and the mutual responsiveness that is essential to constructive help.

Probably no aspect of relationship has been treated more exhaustively than that of involvement. In the professional setting, it implies intervention in its literal meaning of "any interference that may affect the interests of others." It describes a situation in which one person uses his whole self as consciously as possible in the interests of another. These interests may be individual or social in nature. In the professional setting, it is important that they become the concern of someone who possesses knowledge, skill, and sympathy and whose responsibility is to set in motion the helping process.

Helen Harris Perlman describes the interaction that results from this kind of intervention as one in which "a charge or current of feeling must be experienced between two persons. Whether this interaction creates a sense of union or of antagonism, the two persons are for the time 'connected' or 'related' to each other."[22] Perhaps this current, more than any other single factor, embodies the "special elements that are essential in any professional, therapeutic relationship." In her identification of these elements, Perlman includes two that are especially pertinent here: acceptance and purposiveness.

Acceptance is characterized by "warmth and fulness in giving one's self to and receiving another person."

This interchange brings with it the expectation "that the love which is being given will result in some responsive behavior" and, ultimately, will enable a human being "to grow from within himself . . . [and] mold that growth to the prevailing forms of social living." Such expectation is based on the knowledge that every human being reaches out to and seeks the help of another in time of trouble. No matter to whom he turns, the resulting association is emotionally charged; it is dynamic. At the professional level it sparks the interaction that is the starting point of mutual involvement and controlled intervention.

Perlman's description of the process is graphic: "Relationship leaps from one person to the other at the moment when emotion moves between them."[23] She continues with what is, in essence, substantiation of its validity as a medium for the discharge of professional responsibility to the individual in the social order.

> The labors of mind and body involved in problem-solving may feel less arduous when they take place within the warmth and security of a strong relationship; the will to try may be spurred and sustained by the helpfulness and hopefulness it conveys; and far below the surface of consciousness the person may absorb from him to whom he feels related that sense of oneness and yet of separate worth which is the foundation of inner security and self-esteem.[24]

The identifying mark of a relationship such as this is its conscious purposiveness. In contrast to the everyday associations that people take for granted, this one "is formed and maintained for a purpose recognized by both participants, and it ends when that purpose has been

achieved or is judged to be unachievable."[25] This purpose embraces alleviation of all the human needs that are
the focuses of the social worker's knowledge, skill, and
sympathy. The ability to know what to do and how to do
it; the stability to share emotion without becoming emotional; the sensitivity to feel with, not like, the person in
trouble—these are the essentials on which the success of
this purposive relationship depends.

Exercise of Authority

The professional role makes an additional demand upon
social workers, which many seem reluctant to fulfill. This
is a judicious use of the kind of authority that is the
prerogative of the professions. In general, such authority
belongs to anyone who has rights and powers that are
inherent in special knowledge and vested in special functions. Its imposition and its sanctions belong to the moral
or the cultural, rather than the legislative order. Finally,
response to this authority, whether positive or negative,
is a matter of individual choice and one in which the
human being is free of interference in making his decision.

   Nevertheless, when an individual seeks professional
help, he does so because, consciously or unconsciously,
he wants interference in the form of direction. More
important, perhaps, is the fact that he wants this direction
from someone who knows more about the issues than he
does and is, to that extent, different from himself. He
may not realize that this difference is related to the

competence of the specialist rather than to inherent worth. To him, the important fact is that the one who possesses it has the knowledge and the ability to offer a possible solution.

A constructive response demands that the professional person admit his own *plus* value so that he may use it in the interests of another. He thus accepts a position of authority in relation to a person who is essentially like himself and in doing so violates neither the principle of equality nor the virtue of humility. On the contrary, the specialist gives manifest recognition to the inherent dignity of every man whenever he shares his talents—without thought of personal reward—with any man who can benefit from them. This is the essence of humility and respect; it is also the essence of the "authority which infuses the relationship with safety and security and strengthens [the person's] response to guidance"[26] and to love.[27]

In a climate such as this, mutual responsiveness brings about a unity in which the image of each takes shape as one gives of his competence and the other of his burden. Perhaps these images, more than any other factor, account for the eventual co-ordination of thought and action that comes with a meeting of minds and feelings. The result is the kind of involvement in which the problems of one person become the responsibility of both and the difference between the two becomes a resource whose effectiveness depends on its use by each.

As the involvement deepens, the images are sharpened. The social worker's knowledge, skill, and feeling add up to something more than the sum of their respective parts; they are the foundations of a professional relationship. No matter what forces have created a particular problem, the fact remains that the target is a human being who, under stress, reacts not only to need but also to his own feelings about that need. In other words, he reacts with emotion and involvement, not indifference and detachment.

This reaction may range from explosive anger to silent withdrawal, from unrealistic discouragement to equally unrealistic optimism. But whatever form it takes, the response must be accepted as characteristic of man as a unified, integrated, substantive whole. He is not a creature of segmented parts. In the face of difficulty and conflict, reason and emotion follow a collision course; they vie with each other for the domination and control of behavior. The social worker must continuously be alert not only to the objective difficulty that is the immediate concern but also to the emotional response that reflects both past experience and future hopes and fears.

In this kind of mutual recognition and acceptance, the images are perfected and thus supply the media for the mutual responsiveness that belongs to positive relationship. By virtue of this relationship, the helping process, with all its responsibilities and hazards, its compensations and demands, becomes the means whereby social workers fulfill their professional responsibility. In this fulfillment, they become the visible representation—the image—of the ideas and ideals, the goals, and the values that form the quintessence of their role in a democratic social order.

NOTES

1 Howard S. Becker, "The Nature of a Profession," in *Education for the Professions: The Sixty-first Yearbook of the National Society for the Study of Education,* part 2, ed. Nelson B. Henry (Chicago: University of Chicago Press, 1962), p. 38.

2 Ibid., pp. 37-38, 35.

3 Abraham Flexner, "Is Social Work a Profession?" in *Proceedings of the National Conference of Charities and Correction* (Chicago: The Hindmann Company, 1915), pp. 576-90.

4 Mary E. Richmond, "The Need of a Training School in Applied Philanthropy," in *The Long View,* ed. Joanna C. Colcord and Ruth Z.S. Mann (New York: Russell Sage Foundation, 1930), pp. 99-104.

5 John C. Kidneigh, "History of American Social Work," in *Encyclopedia of Social Work,* ed. Henry L. Lurie (New York: National Association of Social Workers, 1965), pp. 3-18.

6 Mary E. Richmond, *Social Diagnosis* (New York: Russell Sage Foundation, 1917).

7 "First Constitution of the American Association of Social Workers," in *The Heritage of American Social Work,* ed. Ralph E. Pum-

180   ENDURING VALUES IN A CHANGING SOCIETY

phrey and Muriel W. Pumphrey (New York: Columbia University Press, 1961), p. 307.

8 *Social Case Work Generic and Specific: An Outline. A Report of the Milford Conference* (New York: American Association of Social Workers, 1929), pp. 3, 15, 17.

9 Edith Abbott, *Social Welfare and Professional Education* (Chicago: University of Chicago Press, 1931), p. 44.

10 Esther Lucile Brown, *Social Work as a Profession,* 4th ed. (New York: Russell Sage Foundation, 1942), p. 22.

11 Charlotte Towle, "The Emotional Element in Learning in Professional Education," in *Professional Education,* five papers delivered at the Twenty-ninth Annual Meeting–American Association of Schools of Social Work, Minneapolis, Minnesota, January 1948 (New York: American Association of Schools of Social Work, 1948), p. 20.

12 Ibid.

13 Ernest V. Hollis and Alice L. Taylor, *Social Work Education in the United States: The Report of a Study Made for the National Council on Social Work Education* (New York: Columbia University Press, 1951), p. 391.

14 Charlotte Towle, *The Learner in Education for the Professions: As Seen in Education for Social Work* (Chicago: University of Chicago Press, 1954), p. 19.

15 Ernest Greenwood, "Attributes of a Profession," *Social Work,* 2(July 1957):45–55.

16 *Code of Ethics* (New York: National Association of Social Workers, 1960), pp. 7–8.

17 Alfred North Whitehead, *Adventures of Ideas* (New York: Macmillan Co., 1933), pp. 71–79.

18 Henry M. Wriston, "The Individual," in *Goals for Americans: Report of the President's Commission on National Goals* (Englewood Cliffs, N.J.: Prentice-Hall, 1960), p. 48.

19 Ibid., p. 50.

20 Substantial progress has been made since this article was written. In early 1975 there were fourteen states (including Puerto Rico) with some form of legal regulation of social work practice.

21 Gordon Hamilton, *Psychotherapy in Child Guidance* (New York: Columbia University Press, 1947), p. 127.

22 Helen Harris Perlman, *Social Casework: A Problem-solving Process* (Chicago: University of Chicago Press, 1957), p. 66.

23 Ibid., pp. 67, 68, 65.

24 Ibid., pp. 65.

25 Ibid., pp. 69.

26 Ibid.

27 Mary J. McCormick, *Diagnostic Casework in the Thomistic Pattern* (New York: Columbia University Press, 1954), pp. 103–25.

8
Mary E. Richmond's Legacy of Values

Mary E. Richmond was born during the first year of the Civil War, and, in her own words, "by the time that I was old enough to realize the kind of world into which I had been dropped, that war was over." As a matter of fact, she had been dropped, as she well knew, into a world of new ideas and ideals, of reforms and reformers, of conflict and sacrifice. Even as a young girl she was sensitive to the varied forces that surrounded her, forces that found common ground only in the common goal of unifying a nation so recently divided against itself.

Many years later, she referred to this "so-called Reconstruction Period" as a "sordid, suspicious, self-seeking time." Along with this indictment, however, she expressed satisfaction that "between the early '90's and the fateful year 1914 . . . there developed in America an entirely new kind of public spirit. Actually, it became difficult for those who could be said to think at all, not to think socially." It was characteristic of Richmond to

This chapter originally appeared in *Social Casework*, October 1961.

rejoice in the fact that during "all that wonderful quarter of a century" she, whose major interest was social work, was able "to appreciate to the full the great advance" because she could remember the earlier time.[1]

Such was the atmosphere social and psychological, in which Richmond's beliefs and convictions took shape and in which her principles, once formulated, were put into practice. The total process found substance and direction in her concept of charity as an absolute value in social work and of self-realization as the goal of every social worker. The same basic value and goal, although known by different names, are recognized currently as intrinsic to the helping process. Their continuing influence on professional performance stands as testimony to the richness of Richmond's legacy to social work and social workers—a legacy made possible by the combination of knowledge and experience, of sensitivity and imagination, that were uniquely hers.

Charity as a Value

The words *charity* and *poverty*—used so sparingly in these days of technical jargon—appear frequently in Richmond's writing. Actually, *charity* is the key word in her analysis of a "reasonable" response to meeting the needs of the poor. Her emphasis on *reasonable* is noteworthy, since reason implies judgment and decision based on facts. This emphasis on facts, as every reader of *Social Diagnosis* well knows, was the key to Richmond's approach to people and their problems.

In her 1899 "Report to the Mayor of Baltimore," Richmond noted,

> It is one of the encouraging signs of the times that men of affairs and men of learning are becoming more and more interested in questions involving the welfare of the poor, that they are "lending their brains out" as well as giving their money, in order to make this a better world for the poor to live in.[2]

During that same year, she elaborated her ideas about the increase of public interest and about the issues that prompted it. In this connection, Richmond described charity as "a great spiritual force" but, too often, a "blind force" that for lack of knowledge and organization found itself "cursing where it would bless, destroying where it would heal." She attributed this unhappy state of affairs to the "complacent way in which people were accustomed to think of their own work and their own good intentions"—to think of themselves rather than of others.[3]

In several of her writings, Richmond expressed the view that such distortion of values could be remedied only by introducing order and objectivity into the method of giving. "We are dealing with human beings, and any lack of efficiency on our part is not merely our loss but theirs." At the same time, she believed that these dealings must reflect the "impulse which makes one anxious to do something for his fellow beings"—that is, the charitable impulse which is "perhaps, the very best thing we have" in a world that "can ill afford to do without the primal instinct of love to our fellow men." Contemporary psychologists may deplore Richmond's seeming fail-

ure to distinguish, technically, between impulse and instinct, but to her, charity or love, irrespective of its origins, meant "sympathetic and patient appreciation of the
lives and aims of creatures least like ourselves." The love
of each for the other, despite "the rapidly widening gulf
between class and class," was the hallmark of constructive giving, and she believed that it must be preserved.

In characteristic fashion, therefore, Richmond proceeded to seek out logical means of preserving this impulse, or instinct, of love. She believed that friendly visiting served this purpose. The leaders in the early charity
organization societies considered such visiting a means of
bridging the gap between rich and poor, and they placed
emphasis on the reciprocal nature of the relationship. In
Richmond's words, the activity was "as helpful to the
well-to-do visitor as to the family visited." She stated that
it was essential that such an activity be marked by "simple
friendliness" and that the "relations with the less fortu-
nate [be] as natural as possible."[4]

In discussing the training of charity workers, Richmond stressed the point that friendly visitors should reflect the "power of sympathy," the quality that in her
scheme of things was "indispensable for the charity
worker." She described it as a sympathy that sprang,
essentially, not from sentimentality, but from "a strong,
deeply rooted sentiment in our charity worker." She did
not view it as an isolated quality or as the gift of a chosen
few. On the contrary, she believed that "if a man is
intelligent, and human, and courageous, and humorous,
and imaginative, it is quite safe to infer that he will be
sympathetic too. Not only will he be sympathetic, but he
will be reasonable." From the practical standpoint, the
problem was to find this paragon of virtues. With her

usual forthrightness, Richmond anticipated the question thus raised: "Now, if you ask me where you are to find any supply of workers with all the qualities I have mentioned, I reply that I have no idea, but surely the first step toward getting what you want is to *know* [italics in original] what you want." Richmond expressed these views about the attributes of a charity worker in 1897.[5]

Fifty years later, Gordon Hamilton discussed the same question against the background, and in the vocabulary, of mid-century psychology and psychiatry. She spoke of caseworkers rather than friendly visitors, and of relationship rather than companionship. In addition, she mentioned a "special kind of love" that is an essential element in the new activity and the new association between the helper and the person receiving help. This love, or acceptance, consists of "warmth, concern, therapeutic understanding, interest in helping the person to get well"—that is, to regain control of his own life and conduct. Hamilton noted that acceptance is characterized by "consistency, neutrality, and firmness"; it is a sincere expression of the caseworker's willingness consciously to enter into and to share in the life experiences of another. According to Hamilton, the question of reciprocity is of minor importance; the essential thing is to recognize the love itself as vital to any real helping.[6]

In 1947, Hamilton placed acceptance at the center of that curious paradox of distance and intimacy that spells "relationship" in present-day casework. A half-century earlier, Richmond had placed the same attribute at the heart of the companionship and friendliness that to her were the epitome of charity. The permanence of values thus becomes apparent as one notes how the helping process of today gained direction and support from the friendly visiting of yesterday.

The Goal of Self-realization

In a paper entitled "The Long View," written in 1919 and first published in 1930, Richmond said the following:

> But we are learning at last that not self-repression but self-realization is the hall-mark of the unselfish life; for it is only by living in a larger whole, and identifying one's self heartily with something quite outside one's own set and one's own personal interests, that self-realization becomes possible.[7]

If that statement were quoted anonymously, it might easily be attributed to a twentieth-century psychiatrist.

Actually, Richmond laid the foundation for the concept of self-realization—without calling it that—as early as 1897. It was then that she formulated, perhaps as much for her own guidance as for the enlightenment of the civic group to which she spoke, the qualifications of paid charity workers. The composite image is worthy of note. First of all, she stated that "one who would succeed in charitable work must be capable of succeeding somewhere else"; in other words, the field has no place for those who have been tried and found wanting. Her second point was that the worker "must have the faculty of taking hold of things by the right handle, a faculty closely allied with a good general education, and yet often divorced from it." Richmond explained her meaning here by saying that one may have "admirable conceptions of society as a whole, and yet be quite unable to deal with the units which compose it."[8]

A few years later, she described what, to her, was an established principle of work:

> It took me a long time to discover that a strong gen-
> eral conviction was not enough in social work, and
> that only by patient study of small details and by an
> application forever renewed of principles to actual
> conditions was progress made.[9]

Other criteria besides a sound education and the
ability to use it were mentioned by Richmond in "The
Training of Charity Workers." She noted that the worker
who measures up must have courage and sympathy. Her
ideas on the latter have already been quoted. Concerning
the former, she recognized two kinds of courage—civic
and personal. She commented that the worker "must be
incapable of 'playing politics'; he must be incorruptible,
even when his civic courage may seem to do temporary
harm to the cause he represents." She added that he can
achieve civic courage through the exercise of personal
courage, through "the ability to say 'no' roundly when
'no' is right."

Richmond stated further, that education, ability,
courage, and sympathy, the four major qualifications of
a charity worker, must in turn be fortified by humor and
imagination. She considered these qualities to be, in their
own way, equally vital to personal growth and stable
performance. Humor, she said, is essential to the courageous man, for courage, by its very nature, can lead a
person into absurd and untenable positions, unless he has
the saving salt of humor. "If he have no sense of humor,
what shall save his sympathy from degenerating into
mere sentimentality? What shall save his theories from
becoming wooden hobbies?"

In regard to imagination, she believed it to be a
"most necessary possession," for without it vision is

myopic. She more than once deplored the fact that charity suffered from this myopia. She explained her concern
by pointing out that those engaged in the work of charity
invariably "have felt keenly enough the misery which is
at hand." However, too often they are seemingly unable
to project themselves and their planning into either the
"cumulative miseries" or the positive gains of the future.
In other words, they can see the trees but not the forest.
What vision they have is not sharp enough or sustained
enough or penetrating enough to influence action and, at
the same time, predict its outcome. In short, they lack the
"picture-making and picture-holding power" that is
imagination. Richmond justified her stand on this point
quite simply. She said, "To say that our charity worker
must have imagination is only another way of saying that
he must be an idealist."[10] She believed that idealism is of
the essence, and added, "In social work it is only the long
views that are cheering."[11]

Since this was the image, the questions facing the
leaders of the period were: How can this image become
a reality? How can it take shape and form in the personality of the social worker? Richmond undoubtedly recognized many possible approaches to such a fulfillment. The
three that she chose for special consideration—experience, education, and cultural pursuits—reflect, unmistak-
ably, her own goals and the values that were part and
parcel of her personality.

Richmond's views on education and experience do
not need to be elaborated; they are evident in all aspects
of her life and work. Her formal education ended when
she finished high school at the age of sixteen; her progress in learning terminated only with her death at the age
of sixty-seven. After she completed high school, she

taught herself shorthand at night, at the end of a twelve-hour working day. She spent evenings and holidays studying the English classics. During the demanding years in Baltimore, she learned to read French. At the age of twenty-one she wrote a paper entitled "Books and Reading"; it reveals her familiarity with the works of De Quincey, Carlyle, Huxley, and Arnold.[12]

Early in 1889, Richmond answered a newspaper advertisement and, as a result, entered what was for her a brave new world. One person already in that world— the world in which the chief concern was human suffering—commented that "she looked pathetically young and she talked like the Ancient of Days." Contrary, perhaps, to the expectations of those around her, she was destined to find her place very quickly among the sages of that world. In less than a decade, she achieved sufficient status to make her plea to the elder statesmen for a revolutionary change—the systematic training of charity workers by means of a structured, educational program. Up to that time, training, such as it was, was achieved through more or less free-floating direct experience with people and their problems. It is easy to imagine Richmond's reaction, both to the method and its results. It is also easy to imagine the reactions of the conservatives among her listeners when, in support of her thesis, she commented in her wry fashion, "Experience, they say, is a good teacher, but some very dull people go to school to her."[13]

Conservatives and nonconservatives alike must have relaxed considerably when it later became apparent that Richmond did not anticipate—much less encourage—the abrupt overthrow of established programs. Not the least among her personal attributes was her ability to see and appreciate a single issue in all its complexities, real and potential, present and future. Her own awareness of this sensitivity once led her to say of herself, "The radicals think I'm a conservative and the conservatives think I'm a radical, and they're both surprised that I somehow manage to keep in the procession."[14] Perhaps Alexander Johnson had the answer to the riddle when, many years later, he said that "even when she was smashing idols . . . she could not help sympathizing with the idolaters."[15]

At any rate, prior to Richmond's first formalized statement on the subject of training, which she made at the National Conference of Charities and Correction, in Toronto, in 1897,[16] she indicated that she expected to labor and to wait. She commented, perhaps a bit wistfully, "If my life is a long one, I hope to see a school of philanthropy too before I die."[17] It is highly probable that no one was more surprised than Richmond herself when, a scant two years later, she found herself lecturing in the newly established Summer School of Applied Philanthropy, the pioneer effort that was destined to become the New York School of Social Work. Professional education had been launched and Mary Richmond was there.

※ The third and, in Richmond's estimation, the most rewarding approach to personal growth was through the world of belles lettres. She herself was genuinely at home with the books that she loved so much. Her reading was always incredibly varied, covering such subjects as meteorology, jurisprudence, biography, electrodynamics —in fact, any subject that was "free from philanthropic taint." As the new century began, she found it increasingly hard to find books of interest. One time, for vaca-

tion reading, she chose several volumes on the weather
and carried them off in triumph, convinced that she had
found "a field where organized charity was not." But she
said, "Never was there a greater mistake. . . . The history
of the Weather Bureau and of the charity organization
movement proved to be as like as two peas." Novels and
essays were even more disappointing. "If you try to escape from philanthropy through light literature, take
warning. The door is barred. Out of ten modern novels
in your trunk, the chances are that nine will be 'sociological.'" This observation has the flavor of Phyllis McGin-
ley's lines about the noted Frenchman: ". . . even white
is partly black/in books by François Mauriac." As for
essays, Richmond commented that they concentrate on
all the old problems under "a thin veil of whimsicality,"
and, she might have added, in the person of a "Screw-
tape" accompanied by his corps of junior devils.[18]

The Value of Poetry

Thus, by a process of elimination, Richmond concluded
that what busy people with scant leisure most need is
more poetry. From this hypothesis, she proceeded to
consider what poetry is and is not. She described it as the
"measured or rhythmic speech" that men use spontane-
ously when "moved by very intimate or by high
thoughts." She called attention to the naturalness of such
speech and cautioned against thinking of it "as an artifi-
cial thing, arbitrarily measured by the caprice of the poet.
In its very essence it is no such thing." By way of exam-

ple, she pointed to the spontaneity and naturalness of the early minstrels, who succeeded in "finding the rhythm which fitted thought [in their songs of love and war] because the rhythm and the thought were related in the very nature of things." It is through this relatedness of thought and expression that poetry "can give us better than anything else, perhaps, a true sense of balance, can keep us wholesome, well-proportioned, all-round people"—the kind of people social workers ought to be.[19]

A quarter of a century later Richmond elaborated her ideas about the relationship of poetry to social work. In "Marginal Notes" she wrote:

> All social workers are dealing . . . with human nature and with the conditions which human nature has created. Could they not deal more successfully if they read more poetry and were able to enter more completely into the spirit behind it?[20]

She answers the question by quoting from one of her favorite poets: "Coleridge says that poetry is a more than usual state of emotion combined with a more than usual order." Richmond commented that this is "a wonderful definition which points the way along which social work must travel." To her the road signs for social work were a sense of order and the power of imagination. Each depends on the other for its proper functioning since each without the other leads to loss of balance. She concluded that social workers could best ensure themselves against such loss by becoming more familiar with the poets and by recognizing the hidden poetry lying beneath even the most sordid things. She noted that in doing so they could not fail to bolster within themselves

the particular kind of insight that brings to intelligent and
sensitive men the added power to understand and serve.

It is possible that similar views about poetry accounted for President Kennedy's summons to Robert
Frost to participate, in the poet's words, "in the august occasion of the State." In commenting on this
participation, one writer referred to Shelley's declaration, "Poets are the unacknowledged legislators of the
world." The writer added that the president seemed
to acknowledge such a role when he extended the invitation and again when, sometime after his inaugura-
tion, he remarked, "I think politicians and poets share
at least one thing, and that is that their greatness depends upon the courage with which they meet the
challenges of life."[21]

It seems safe to say that Mary Richmond would
have approved of Robert Frost's appearance at the
inaugural ceremony and of the sentiment that
prompted the invitation. She would have been quick
to understand the bond between the venerable word
artist and the youthful world leader. She might have
found the explanation of that bond in the magnificent
stanza with which Edna St. Vincent Millay concluded
her "Renascence":

> The world stands out on either side
> No wider than the heart is wide;
> Above the world is stretched the sky,—
> No higher than the soul is high.
> The heart can push the sea and land
> Farther away on either hand;
> The soul can split the sky in two,
> And let the face of God shine through.

But East and West will pinch the heart
That cannot keep them pushed apart;
And he whose soul is flat—the sky
Will cave in on him by and by.[22]

NOTES

1 Mary E. Richmond, "The Long View," in *The Long View*, ed. Joanna C. Colcord and Ruth Z.S. Mann (New York: Russell Sage Foundation, 1930), p. 468.

2 Richmond, "Report to the Mayor of Baltimore," in *The Long View*, ed. Colcord and Mann, p. 130.

3 Richmond, "What Is Charity Organization?" in *The Long View*, ed. Colcord and Mann, pp. 131–32.

4 Richmond, "The Friendly Visitor," in *The Long View*, ed. Colcord and Mann, p. 41.

5 Richmond, "The Training of Charity Workers," in *The Long View*, ed. Colcord and Mann, pp. 88–89.

6 Gordon Hamilton, *Psychotherapy in Child Guidance* (New York: Columbia University Press, 1947), pp. 126–27.

7 Richmond, "The Long View," in *The Long View*, ed. Colcord and Mann, p. 469.

8 Richmond, "The Training of Charity Workers," in *The Long View*, ed. Colcord and Mann, p. 87.

9 Richmond, "The Settlement and Friendly Visiting," in *The Long View*, ed. Colcord and Mann, pp. 121–22.

10 Richmond, "The Training of Charity Workers," in *The Long View*, ed. Colcord and Mann, pp. 88–89.

11 Richmond, "A Background for the Art of Helping," in *The Long View*, ed. Colcord and Mann, p. 583.

12 Richmond, "Books and Reading," in *The Long View*, ed. Colcord and Mann, pp. 19–28.

13 Richmond, "The Training of Charity Workers," in *The Long View*, ed. Colcord and Mann, p. 95.

14 Introduction to *The Long View*, ed. Colcord and Mann, p. 15.

15 Alexander Johnson, "An Apotheosis of Case Work: The Long View, *"The Family*, 11(February 1931):331.

16 Richmond, "The Need of a Training School in Applied Philanthropy," in *The Long View*, ed. Colcord and Mann, pp. 99–104.

17 Richmond, "The Training of Charity Workers," in *The Long View*, ed. Colcord and Mann, p. 90.

18 Richmond, "Vacation Notes of an Idle Philanthropist," in *The Long View*, ed. Colcord and Mann, p. 163.

19 Richmond, "A Plea for Poetry," in *The Long View*, ed. Colcord and Mann, pp. 148–50.

20 Richmond, "Marginal Notes," in *The Long View*, ed. Colcord and Mann, p. 509.

21 Bette Richart, "Poets on the New Frontier," *The Commonweal*, 74(May 12, 1961):175.

22 Edna St. Vincent Millay, "Renascence," from *Collected Poems* (New York: Harper & Row, 1917, 1975). Reprinted by permission of Norma Millay Ellis.

360
m 131

102842